Working with Violence and Confrontation Using Solution Focused Approaches

by the same author

Children and Young People Whose Behaviour is Sexually Concerning or Harmful
Assessing Risk and Developing Safety Plans
Jackie Bateman and Judith Milner
ISBN 978 1 84905 361 7
eISBN 978 0 85700 714 8

Working with Children and Teenagers Using Solution Focused Approaches
Enabling Children to Overcome Challenges and Achieve their Potential
Judith Milner and Jackie Bateman
ISBN 978 1 84905 082 1
eISBN 978 0 85700 261 7

of related interest

Mediation Skills and Strategies
A Practical Guide
Tony Whatling
Foreword by Mohamed M. Keshavjee
ISBN 978 1 84905 299 3
eSIBN 978 0 85700 627 1

Engaging with Perpetrators of Domestic Violence
Practical Techniques for Early Intervention
Kate Iwi and Chris Newman
ISBN 978 1 84905 380 8
eIBSN 978 0 85700 738 4

Changing Offending Behaviour
A Handbook of Practical Exercises and Photocopiable Resources for Promoting Positive Change
Clark Baim and Lydia Guthrie
Foreword by Fergus McNeill
ISBN 978 1 84905 511 6
eISBN 978 0 85700 928 9

From Violence to Resilience
Positive Transformative Programmes to Grow Young Leaders
Jo Broadwood and Nic Fine
ISBN 978 1 84905 183 5
eISBN 978 0 85700 314 0

Working with Gangs and Young People
A Toolkit for Resolving Group Conflict
Jessie Feinstein and Nia Imani Kuumba
ISBN 978 1 84310 447 6
eISBN 978 1 84642 522 6

Working with Violence and Confrontation Using Solution Focused Approaches

Creative Practice with Children, Young People and Adults

Judith Milner and Steve Myers

Jessica Kingsley *Publishers*
London and Philadelphia

First published in 2017
by Jessica Kingsley Publishers
73 Collier Street
London N1 9BE, UK
and
400 Market Street, Suite 400
Philadelphia, PA 19106, USA

www.jkp.com

Library of Congress Cataloging in Publication Data
A CIP catalog record for this book is available from the Library of Congress.

British Library Cataloguing in Publication Data
A CIP catalogue record for this book is available from the British Library.

ISBN 978 1 78592 055 4
eISBN 978 1 78450 312 3

Printed and bound in Great Britain

*Nick Lofthouse, for his commitment to maintaining
the safety of others at the risk of his own*

*We would like to thank David Bottomley for tolerance,
patience and his grounded approach*

Contents

1. Introduction 9
Solution focused approaches 13
Solution focused explanations for violent behaviour 21
Resilience. 24
The Signs of Safety approach. 25

2. Understanding the Position of Each Person. 27
Respectfulness 27
Problem-free talk 31
Listening 32
Building partnership 34
Talking with people who can't or won't talk 35
Do's for constructive conversations 39
Don'ts for constructive conversations 41

3. Finding Exceptions or Unique Outcomes to
Violence and Conflict 43
Separating the person from the problem 49
Where exceptions are relevant to the problem. 52
Where the exceptions don't seem relevant 54
Where there are no exceptions at all 57
Recording signs of safety 57
Conclusion 62

4. Setting Achievable Goals 63
Defining goals 63
Setting safety goals 65
Preferred futures 69
The miracle question 72
Group miracle questions 76
Shortened circular miracle question. 77
Where the problem is denied 78

Where there are conflicting goals 80
People with learning difficulties 84

5. Discovering Strengths and Resources 85
Turning deficits into resources 85
Starting a strengths conversation 88
Strengths in adversity 92
Complicating stories 94
Group strengths and resources 94
Finding strengths in people who are socially isolated 96
Strengths that build safety 98

6. Scaling Safety and Progress 102
Scaling questions 102
Scaled questions for safety goal setting 104
Questions for assessing safety 106
Questions that assess likelihood of change 110
Assessing progress 112
Being creative 121

7. Ending a Session 124
Deciding on tasks 124
Evaluating the session and ending it 130
Feedback 132
Subsequent sessions 137
When things are better 137
When things are the same 139
When things are worse 141
When things are mixed 143

8. Groupwork 144
Using connections 144
Advantages of groupwork 144
Setting up a group 145
Determining group rules 147
Groupwork practice principles 149
Managing difficult group members 153
Flexible groupwork in testing situations 155
Forgotten victims 157

REFERENCES 158

INDEX 162

Chapter 1

Introduction

We all have vast personal experience of violence, whether this be the sudden shock when your toddler bites you, the emotional violence of being shunned by your fellow pupils, receiving an abusive text or being sexually harassed at work.

It is highly likely that you will also have *perpetrated* violence, whether this be the time you smacked your child, joined in with emotional bullying at school, put down a colleague at work, used language to subtly intimidate others or used your position to get your own way.

From these experiences we know that violence pervades our lives in many complex ways and that we all have the capacity to be violent in certain circumstances at the same time as we are vulnerable to violence being done to us in different circumstances. Sometimes we feel powerful and in control, other times we feel helpless and lacking control. And it's not necessarily a difference in strength or status that defines whether we are victim or victimiser; for example, a defiant child has the potential to demolish parental competence and control.

When we are faced with responding to violence in our work, we have a tendency to identify saints and sinners, victims and offenders, adults and children, and this is reflected in the literature. First, there are books telling you how to work with children who are violent (mostly parenting manuals), although books on how to work with adults who are violent tend to be mostly about how to handle males (mostly groupwork). Second, there are books on how to respond to the victims of violence and these are mainly children, females and elders (mostly individual counselling). As you know, life is much more complicated than this, and the situations that face you at work are not easily disentangled.

PRACTICE ACTIVITY 1.1

After Scott's parents split up, he lived with his mother and two older brothers. After he was sexually abused by the elder brother, Adrian, who was promptly ejected from the home, there were unsubstantiated allegations of further abuse by his other brother, Alan, so Scott was sent to live with his father and his new family. He has been happy with this arrangement, although he doesn't get on with his stepsister, Ellie, who is also 15 years old. He has been discovered in bed with his 7-year-old stepsister, Anna. When questioned, he confessed to abusing both Anna and his 10-year-old step brother, Dominic. He blamed Anna for getting into bed with him and inviting him to 'touch' her. Anna freely admitted that she had done this and it then emerged that Scott and Anna had been sexually abused by a family friend who used Scott's need to escape from the 'bother' Ellie created for him, and Anna's willingness to please, as a means to groom them. Ellie, Anna and Dominic have all been diagnosed as having some degree of autism, Dominic being most severely affected.

The family friend has been prosecuted and received a lengthy prison sentence. Scott has been returned to his mother's home under strict bail conditions. He has contact with his step siblings at weekends, supervised by his father and stepmother. At home, he is supervised by his brother, Alan, who is still living at home. At school, he is supervised by nominated staff.

Scott wants more freedom to go to a youth club in the evening and also see more of his step siblings. Dominic and Anna find it difficult to understand why he's not allowed to live with them. None of the children are showing any symptoms of trauma – other than Anna, whose sexualised behaviour is causing concern: she masturbates openly at home, and at school she makes overtures to other pupils at playtime.

- How would you respond in this situation if you were Scott's form tutor or Dominic's special-needs adviser or Anna's form teacher or the child protection social worker or the youth-club worker?

- Have you any concerns about Alan and Ellie?

(Adapted from Myers and Milner 2007, p.112)

Other than violence involving attacks on strangers, it is often impossible to delineate one person a victim and one a victimiser – even when there is an obvious power differential. For example, Doreen visited her frail 92-year-old mother almost daily to do the tasks her mother found too difficult: cleaning, preparing hot meals, laying the coal fire and doing the washing – despite a distinct lack of gratitude from her mother. She visited her mother's care manager one day, tearfully recounting that her mother had tried to strangle her as she laid the fire. She was badly shaken by the assault and also resentful: 'I'm 67 myself and I planned to spend my retirement seeing more of my grandchildren not have to put up with more of mum's criticisms. And now this'. Similarly, in our work with domestic violence, we found that although one person may be the one who is responsible for the physical violence, the other partner is often found to be emotionally abusive, and that this is true not only of male-on-female violence but also female-on-male violence and same-sex violence (Milner and Jessop 2003; Milner and Singleton 2008). The complexities of intimate relationships make it difficult to decide who should be punished and who should receive treatment, and how risk is to be managed.

There are many different explanations for violence that are based on preferred theories, research, ideology and experience, and each of them has some merit in particular situations or circumstances. We all bring our individual ways of understanding the world to making sense of social phenomena such as violence, be they psychological (he is a psychopath), biological (it is his testosterone), sociological (it is usual for his class), cultural (she has become a crude, boisterous drinker) or political (she has been indoctrinated), or sometimes a combination of all of them. Consider the practice activity below.

PRACTICE ACTIVITY 1.2

Ahmed is a Somali-heritage 15-year-old boy who has been raised by his refugee single mother in an area of inner-city deprivation. His violent father left the family when Ahmed was 5 years old and he was subsequently sexually abused by one of his mother's new partners. He has always struggled behaviourally and academically at school and has been diagnosed as having an anxious-avoidant attachment disorder, attention-deficit hyperactivity disorder, intermittent explosive disorder, dyslexia and dyspraxia. He has been part of a local gang since the age of 8 years, taking part in various criminal activities involving drugs and firearms. Ahmed is a regular and heavy cannabis user. He has been arrested for a joint attack on a member of a different gang which resulted in the victim losing an eye. Ahmed maintains that the victim racially abused him and that the attack was justified.

- What different explanations are there for Ahmed's violent behaviour?
- How would you go about addressing this behaviour with him?
- What would you choose to talk about first?

We have no doubt that anyone reading this will recognise that there are a myriad of ways in which this violent behaviour can be understood, and each of these ways will be more or less attractive to readers depending on their preferred theoretical construct of the world. Each of these ways will also have relevant research that can be called upon to support the explanation and have interventions that can be applied to respond to the violence. So, for example, Ahmed may be viewed as in need of long-term psychotherapy to resolve the abuse he experienced as a child which has impacted on his core being; he may be seen as requiring cognitive restructuring to repair the damaged ways in which his brain has been 'wired' so that he can respond more appropriately to situations; he may need to change how he expresses his masculinity, or he may benefit from pharmacological therapies to control his diagnoses.

The commonality with all these approaches is that they share a desire to explain and categorise the behaviour so that the appropriate interventions can be made to address the problem. They presume that there is a 'deficit' in the person that requires expert diagnosis and technical adjustment to resolve it. This deficit can be due to the person's biology, childhood experiences or social learning, but the assumption is that something is not right and needs changing. This places the worker in a very powerful position of knowing more about the violent behaviour than the person who has it, bringing their knowledge to enable the person to truly understand why they behave in this way and what needs to be done to deal with it.

These approaches are generally keen to create labels for 'types' of violent people, grouping people together into categories that can then be given the correct treatment to deal with the problem. An example of this is when someone who has been violent is sent on an anger management programme which consists of a set number of sessions that are designed to challenge and change the disordered thinking that people have about situations where they are violent. This group approach presumes that the participants have similar characteristics based on the violent behaviour and that these are amenable to the same intervention. They have been defined by their behaviour and this is the focus of the work to be done, leading to interventions that are standardised and follow a formula. The complexity of the individual (who they are, what their motivation for the behaviour was and so forth) is less important than their identity as being a *type* of violent person, so this approach tends to reduce the person to their unwanted problematic behaviour and to prescribe specific ways of managing this.

There are similarities here with medical diagnoses, where symptoms are observed, categorised and diagnosed, and then the appropriate treatment is prescribed. This presumes that the behaviour can be treated as a disease and all that is required is the correct medicine in the right dosage to eradicate the problem. If we read, for example, cognitive behavioural treatment (CBT) as the 'correct medicine' and determine ten sessions as the 'right dosage', then we get a sense of how this model works. The person is labelled as violent and is treated in the same way as other violent people.

Solution focused approaches

Solution focused approaches differ from other ways of working in that the focus is on understanding solutions to work toward a problem-free future rather than understanding problems, which underpins the approaches outlined previously. It has similar values to humanist counselling and some of the cognitive and behavioural questioning and task-setting of CBT (for an overview see Myers and Milner 2007), but avoids the categorisation and treatment allocation model of problem-oriented approaches.

A solution focused approach considers language and context to be crucial in how we understand and engage with the person, and in this it can be seen as located within poststructuralist, postmodern or social constructionist thinking (see Myers 2008), influenced by the writing of Derrida (1973) and Wittgenstein (1980). This means that the person is viewed as someone who has *agency*, that is, having the ability to be more than just the stories that are told about them through their given identity. Culture and society are seen as very important, and they influence how we make sense of ourselves and our situations, including how we construct the very idea of an inner world. Indeed, O'Connell (2001, p.29) says that a solution focused approach does not focus on some notion of 'an inner world divorced from a cultural, anthropological context' but rather examines 'what lies *between* people, i.e. an interactional perspective', which is much more fluid and open to change and interpretation than fixed ideas of the self. It also recognises the importance of the social world in influencing how we go about changing behaviour.

An example of how language use influences practice with violence is in the changing terminology used to describe children with sexual misbehaviours. Bateman and Milner (2015) discuss how using language such as 'young sex offender', 'sexual abuser' or even 'mini-perpetrator' fixes the identity of the young person as a sex offender with all the weight of negativity associated with this label. The young person is viewed as the problem, and the focus is on dealing with their deficits that have led to the behaviour. The young person can internalise the image of themselves as a sex offender through practices such as CBT which demand vigilance against the feelings, thoughts and situations that may trigger their abusive behaviour: they are 'wired' to offend and need to guard against this. In recognition of the consequences of using such language, there has been a move to develop terms that have a different perspective. So, language such as 'children with sexually harmful or concerning behaviours' or 'young people with sexually problematic behaviours' refocuses onto the unwanted *behaviour* rather than the young person, reinforcing that it is the sexually harmful behaviours that are the problem rather than the young person themselves. This creates more space for change, as it is easier to imagine change (and therefore to achieve it) when we think of *behaviour* as opposed to *identity*.

Solution focused approaches have their roots in counselling and have developed from the work of Steve de Shazer, the Milwaukee Centre for Brief Therapy and Solution Focused Brief Therapy (SFBT). SFBT claimed to have identified the key processes involved in successful therapeutic interventions by analysing the research evidence, including finding that therapy did not always have to be long term to be effective enough to make a difference, hence 'brief'. de Shazer (1988) identified that many solutions to problems were often actually supporting the problem, so he explored the ways in which problems were unstable, that is, when they were different and when they were less of a problem. By seeing problems as fluid and changeable rather than fixed and either present or absent, he was able to bring in a more nuanced understanding of how workable solutions could be developed. Understanding those times when things were working well provides the material for co-constructing a problem-free future, and this is based on the experience of the person rather than the professional's prescription of what needs to be done.

A solution focused model fits well with the broader strengths-based approach of Dennis Saleebey (2013), which is optimistic about the willingness and ability of people to change their lives for the better and to play a constructive and valued role in society. (For an overview of this, see Milner, Myers and O'Byrne 2015.) The theoretical underpinning of strengths-based approaches is social constructionism that has been identified by Burr (2003) as a critical stance toward 'scientific' knowledge taken for granted on the grounds that social 'facts' change over time and in different cultural contexts. Such knowledge may be helpful to some groups of people but positively oppressive to other groups. It is deeply sceptical about the ability of the grand modernist theories and explanations to deliver truth – holding to a plurality of truths, including those contained in the 'local' theories of people. Therefore, it avoids any form of diagnostic labelling and sees professional categorisation of people as disempowering, preferring to view people as having capabilities that need to be recognised and developed. Milner and Myers (2007, p.132) give the example of a young person with sexually concerning behaviour who was considered a particular risk by his teachers because he had been diagnosed as suffering from Asperger's syndrome, and because of this was presumed to be unable to show empathy for his victims. He was viewed by his solution focused practitioner as having special strengths: his tendency to 'intellectualise' his behaviour was harnessed to assist him to analyse it and develop a solution that had meaning for him.

Practitioners using a solution focused approach take a 'not knowing' stance toward the person they are working with, a position that requires the worker to remain curious and continue to ask questions, rather than closing down the conversations when we think we have found 'the answer'. Such a stance reduces the possibility that workers are imposing their own views, explanations and preferred theoretical perspectives on people, ensuring that there is the best chance of hearing what the person has to say and how they make sense of their situation. As Clark helpfully stated, 'Why do we construct solutions solely from our point of view, when we are not the ones being asked to change' (2013, p.134). Workers ask questions about difference, that is, what was happening differently when the problem was less of a problem and what would need to be different for the problem to be less in the future. Indeed, solution focused conversations avoid dwelling on the problem as this is not what needs talking about; the conversation is about solutions. As Miller describes it, 'Stories that only emphasize giving up troublesome behaviours actually direct clients' attention to that which they are supposed to avoid' (1997, p.75), so even talking about ending the problem highlights and focuses on the problem. Solution focused practitioners would use this time to talk about solutions instead, becoming what Sharry, Madden and Darmody (2012) describe as 'solution detectives', looking for people's strengths and resources that are helpful in creating a problem-free future.

Solution focused practice sees the problem as outside the person: the person is not the problem; the problem is the problem. The practitioner joins with the person *against* the problem and thereby gets a different story, avoiding pathologising the person or concentrating on their deficits. This solution focused approach seeks to find the seeds of solutions in the person's experience, seeking those occasions or *exceptions*, however small or rare, when the problem is less acute in order to identify when and how that person is doing or thinking something different that alleviates the problem. This involves listening carefully to, and then *utilising*, what the person brings to the encounter, focusing on problem-free moments, constructing an imagined future when the problem is no longer there, and getting a very detailed description from the person of what will be different then and whether any of that is already beginning to happen. In partnership, the person and the practitioner build a picture of a possible future without the problem. We consider this approach to be fundamentally anti-oppressive as it is about empowering the voice and experience of the person.

Emotions are not ignored but they are validated through what O'Hanlon (1995) has referred to as *empathy with a twist*, adding a word that implies a possibility of difference. For example, if someone says he feels suicidal, the practitioner could reply, 'That must be scary, have you felt suicidal *before*?' If the answer is affirmative, the follow-up question could be, 'How did you recover *last time*?' (Lipchik 2000). People need to be heard but, rather than attempting to understand their emotional experiences as separate, emotion, cognition and behaviour are viewed as interdependent and the focus is on engaging at an emotional level (Lipchik and Turnell 1999). Hence, the person is asked how they *do* depression, happiness, being calm and so forth (i.e. actions over which they can gain some control), rather than how they *feel* them (i.e. emotions over which they have little control).

A solution focused approach is different from most other ways of understanding violence. Rather than assuming that information about a problem will help in finding its solution, the assumption is that we can understand a solution without necessarily knowing a great deal about the problem. Searching for an understanding of a problem usually leads to a list of deficits or negatives, whereas this approach says that what is needed is a list of personal strengths, resources and exceptions to the problem. Lists of deficits often risk overwhelming both people and the practitioners, engendering hopelessness and a tendency on the part of the practitioner to use such expressions as 'unmotivated', 'resistant' or 'not ready to change'. In a solution focused approach, 'resistance' is regarded as an inability on the part of the worker to recognise the person's 'unique way of cooperating' and an indication that more careful listening needs to happen. The presumption is that the worker and the person haven't *yet* found the best way to communicate. Of course, the complexities of violence mean that some people actually enjoy their behaviour as it can give emotional and social rewards, which makes change harder to achieve especially if the change process is linked to the development of shame and/or guilt.

PRACTICE EXAMPLE 1.1

Nineteen-year-old Carl describes a recent fight he started:

It's like a popular idea but I do see red. Round the outside and the person I'm going for and that's all I see. One minute I could see you all normal but then I couldn't see behind you and just see red and the part I'm aiming for. I hit. Draw blood. Seeing blood doesn't bother me. I like them on the deck because then I know I've done it right. I also walk into gang fights...or create one. We were skating. I'm good at ice skating and we were doing these turns. This lad got in my way and I ice sprayed him as I turned. He effed and blinded (i.e. used expletives) and then one of his mates spat in my face. I nodded to my best mate and we got a gang together, went speed skating after them. I speed skated right up to him, nutted him, jumped up and started kicking him with my blades on. I didn't feel it at the time but I was cut to ribbons. Broken knuckles, blood coming out of my ears, my legs slashed to pieces. All my mates waded in.

Then we had to have a police escort out of the place, the others had rounded up a gang and were waiting for us when we came out. I got a right buzz off of it. I were laughing halfway through...after, I think, I wish I could go again, feel sort of...smug satisfaction. It was a real high. I do a lot of stuff...some I can remember, some I have to be told. Usually by a copper afterwards.

(Milner and O'Byrne 2002, p.106)

A solution focused approach does not have an explanation for violent behaviour, nor does it attempt to predict dangerousness. This is in part because it considers that diagnoses provide extremely limited perspectives of individuals' capacities for change. It is particularly concerned with the negative effects of labelling; for example, Turnell and Edwards (1999) argue that violence in families usually accounts for no more than 5% of the family's behaviour and that focusing solely on this ignores the 95% of family competence. Concentrating on the signs of danger not only gives an unbalanced picture, but engaging with risk leads to defensiveness, engendering an adversarial and hostile relationship (Berg 1994; Lipchik and Kubicki 1996).

By not holding one, or more, explanations for violent behaviour, the solution focused practitioner is acknowledging that *accurate* prediction of violent behaviour is out of our reach. For example, although research has identified links between violent behaviour and psychopathy, Gondolf and White's (2001) study of 840 male participants in partner-batterer programmes in the US found that the evidence of psychopathic disorder was relatively low, particularly in 'repeat assaulters', of whom 60% showed no serious personality dysfunction or psychopathology. This fits with some feminist accounts of male domestic violence as systematic and 'normal' masculine behaviour. Also, while the 'repeat assaulters' were likely to be younger, have substance abuse problems and to have been arrested for other criminal offences (similar in findings to the Royal College of Psychiatrists' study, 1996), the extent of difference in these problems was small and not clinically significant. The differences between reoffenders and other participants are not substantial enough to help professionals predict or identify high-risk offenders. Any assumption that people who are violent are similar to each other and different from non-violent people is, therefore, fatally flawed. Additionally, negative assumptions about the meaning of the offender's behaviour means that situational and complex variables that might be significant are ignored (Lee, Sebold and Uken 2003). The 'Power and Control Wheel',[1] for example, is common in treating men who are domestically violent, and it is predicated on the assumption that men abuse their power over women, with triggers, cycles and supporting beliefs that require strong challenge. This particular approach may not be appropriate for all men as it presumes there is one way of being a man and that this requires changing, rather than exploring the complexities of intimate partner violence. Different masculinities or the realities of violence are not addressed through this approach, which is why it does not make sense when applied to same-sex or female-on-male violence. Social responses to violence tend to lean toward punishing men and providing women with therapy, indicating that men are viewed as 'bad' and women as 'mad', which demonstrates how gender is used to understand an individual's violence.

PRACTICE EXAMPLE 1.2

Sixteen-year-old Karen had been in intensive care for a week after one fight, a fate she had delivered to another girl some weeks earlier. The fighting was second hand: Karen had beaten up her 'victim' as a favour for a friend and had been beaten up in turn by two 'hard cases' employed by her 'victim'. Despite the constant fear of retaliation, Karen found fighting exciting:

I go for weak people because I know it hurts them more...like I was hurt. It's a bit scary at the start, I get butterflies in my stomach and then start shaking. Then I get this...this sort of adrenalin rush. I like to see blood. When the blood runs, that's the best bit. I feel satisfied then.

(Adapted from Milner 2001, p.78)

This is not to say that accountability is either denied or minimised in a solution focused approach to violent behaviour; what is avoided is blame and confrontation. In the first place, 'acknowledgement, while preferable, is neither a sufficient nor a necessary condition of safety' (Turnell and Edwards 1999, p.140); we all know of heavy drinkers who acknowledged the mantra 'I am an alcoholic' but went on drinking, or the serial sex offender who acknowledges his crimes

---

1   Website: www.theduluthmodel.org

during a prison sentence but reoffends on release. The motivation of a violent offender to acknowledge culpability and guilt may be to avoid a long prison sentence or obtain parole, while denial may be due to shame, the desire to maintain an interpersonal relationship or a way of avoiding humiliation. Many violent offenders are not able to discuss their violence in detail until they have gained some confidence in their ability to be different (Milner and Jessop 2003; Milner 2004a). Equally, the idea that confrontation will help offenders see the error of their ways, and that they have to accept responsibility for past behaviour before they can move forward, is not particularly effective. It takes considerable effort and usually results in the creation of significant resistance. This has the potential to turn the therapeutic relationship into an adversarial and punitive one. Here there is an assumption that violent offenders are in denial (see, for example, Teft 1999), or ambivalent about making changes in their lives (Miller and Rollnick 2002). Importantly, being accountable and taking responsibility for past behaviour does not necessarily help people to ascertain what they need to do differently.

The solution focused practitioner holds violent offenders responsible for finding their own solutions to their behaviour, particularly what their futures will be like when they are violence free. However, there is no assumption made that this will be easy; solution building is a process that requires discipline and effort. The role of the solution focused practitioner is, therefore, one of helping the offender define a goal that is achievable, measurable and ethical; helping them find exceptions to the violent behaviour; and helping to find solution behaviours, and then amplifying, supporting and reinforcing these behaviours. Exceptions are not discovered simply to be praised, nor are solution behaviours regarded as 'positives'; rather, they are examined as possible competencies that the person can utilise in the search for a satisfactory and enduring solution. For example, if a person can give an example of a time when they were calm in a situation that has led to violence previously, they are asked where and how they did this, and if they can do it again.

As Durrant (1993) puts it, most psychological approaches tend to assume that qualities are measurable entities, that there are 'normative' criteria for determining healthy functioning and that we need to identify deficit and fault before planning intervention. He contrasts this with the solution focused approach, which assumes that

(a) the meaning of behaviour and emotion is relative and constructed, (b) psychological and emotional characteristics are partly a product of the observer's assessment and interpretation, (c) intervention need not be directly related to the problem and (d) practitioners should build on strengths rather than attempt to repair deficits. This approach therefore develops an apparently 'atheoretical, non-normative, client determined view' (Berg and Miller 1992, p.5) of difficulties in which change is regarded as constant and inevitable. As a result, it makes sense to find what bits of positive change are happening and to use them to develop a solution. If practitioners do not look carefully for what the client is doing when the problem is not happening, or is not perceived to be a problem, these exceptions will go unnoticed. The most striking example of this is the 'pre-session change' question. Because de Shazer's (1991) team believe that change is constant, that no problem, mood or behaviour happens all the time or to the same degree, new clients are asked what has changed since the appointment was arranged. The team found that a considerable proportion of people reported some change. By then asking 'How did you do that?', they quickly got a solution focused assessment under way.

Solution focused explanations for violent behaviour

Quite simply, solution focused brief practice does not have an explanation for violent behaviour, nor does it attempt to predict risk. By not imposing explanations, the solution focused practitioner acknowledges that accurate prediction is out of our reach; the high risk doesn't always happen and low risk sometimes does. Instead, a bespoke response is provided, one that regards each person as unique with their own unique solution. Solution focused practice rests on a number of important assumptions:

- Assumptions about problems
  - The problem is the problem; the person is not the problem.
  - Problems do not necessarily indicate a personal deficit.
  - Problems happen in interactions between people rather than inside them.
  - Problems are not always present; exceptions occur.

    ◦   Complicated problems do not always require a complicated solution.

(Myers 2007, pp.32–33)

Sean, who is 12 years old, has problems with his temper and becomes violent at school. He described his temper as being the 'red mist' that descends on him and leads to the violent behaviour. We were then able to draw a picture of the 'red mist' and look at it, puzzling over what made it stronger and what it didn't like, developing ideas for reducing the impact of the 'red mist' and his violent behaviour.

- Assumptions about the past

  ◦ Events just happen: exploring the past leads to blame, whereas the goal is to develop responsibility for the future.

  ◦ Exploring a problem-free future avoids having to dwell on or understand the past.

  ◦ A diagnosis does not have to determine the future.

Sharon had had a very difficult childhood with many damaging experiences and had been diagnosed with borderline personality disorder. She had lost her temper when on a night out with friends and hit someone. Sharon decided that she would like to focus on avoiding violent behaviour and being sociable, as she could not change her past and previous attempts to 'come to terms with it' had led to misery, but she *could* make an attempt to take control of her future.

- Assumptions about change

  ◦ Change always happens; nothing stays the same.

  ◦ What may appear to be small changes can be hugely significant.

  ◦ Change can be constructed through talk.

Charles had been bullying colleagues at work by using his large size to physically dominate and using bad language to intimidate. He maintained that people provoked him and that he was justified in his actions. Following disciplinary action he was given counselling where he was able to identify that he had already been in a situation which would previously have led him to behave inappropriately but he had 'bitten his tongue' and kept quiet. This provided the basis for a discussion about how he managed to do this and how he could do it again.

- Assumptions about talking

  ○ Hearing what the person has to say is important.

  ○ Take a not-knowing stance that reduces premature and imposed worker judgement.

  ○ Stay on the surface of conversations rather than looking beneath; any search for meaning is likely to be the worker's interpretation.

  ○ People experience and make sense of their world in different ways; their reality may not be yours.

James had a consultation with Debbie, a psychotherapist, about his aggressive behaviour toward his partner. Debbie asked questions about his childhood and experiences of being parented. She found that he had the symptoms of an anxious-preoccupied attachment disorder and that theory and research indicated that this was likely to be the result of an abusive childhood. Debbie advised that this condition would require intensive long-term psychotherapy to resolve the difficulties caused by his underlying emotional working model. James felt that he had had a normal upbringing but accepted that his single working mother may have been responsible for his current inability to control his behaviour by depriving him of the necessary time and affection to develop a secure attachment. However, he felt that his aggression was related to the stress he was experiencing due to the threat of redundancy at work.

- Assumptions about solutions

  ○ Identify what is going right rather than what is going wrong.

  ○ People have the solutions to the problems; assist them in finding these solutions.

- ○ Solutions generated by the person are more likely to be meaningful, achievable and successful.

- ○ Imposing what works for others does not always work for the individual; seek what works for the individual.

- ○ Increasing people's choices will enable behaviour change.

- ○ Goals need to be meaningful for the person in order to be successful, but they also need to be legal and moral.

With some encouragement Lawrence was able to see that he was actually very good at football. He used his footballing skills of determination, fearlessness and team playing to build up his resistance to the bullying he was experiencing by not responding to the taunts about his sexuality and calling on trusted friends to support him. This was preferable to the violence he had been using previously. His goal in life had been to be financially secure and respected through becoming a successful drug dealer like his older brother, so his worker agreed with him that it would be better to be financially secure and respected through becoming a professional footballer.

Resilience

In the strengths-based approach resilience is defined as the ability to adapt successfully in the face of adversity (Anderson 2013). Resilience is a capacity that we all have and can be tapped into to make a positive and powerful contribution to the lives of people: 'all individuals, regardless of how debilitated or hopeless can dig deep enough to find and summon strengths in themselves that they may never have tapped before or thought existed' (Benard and Truebridge 2013, p.205). People who are violent need to be resilient against their violent behaviour, taking appropriate responsibility for themselves and using their resources to work toward a violence-free future. Violence can occur when people feel hopeless or when there is little motivation to behave otherwise, so exploring and developing resilience is a useful exercise.

The emphasis in this model is on the skills and characteristics that make some people more resilient than others (Reivich and Shatte 2003; Selekman 2002, 2007). Some people cope with setbacks very well, whether they are small ones, such as not being picked for the football team, or big ones, such as living in a home where there is domestic violence. Their resilience helps them pick themselves up and get on with life. A growing body of research and practice shows that most people overcome serious adversity; particularly demanding and stressful experiences do not lead inevitably to vulnerability, failure to adapt and psychopathology (for an overview, see Saleebey 2013). Others don't cope as well; they get stuck, see life as very unfair and sometimes become depressed or begin harming themselves or others. The difference between these two groups of people is not the severity of their problems; it is the ability to get a good outcome in the face of adversity. Research on resilience has argued for a shift in our attention from the traditional focus on an individual's deficits to engaging individuals in the identification of strengths within times of difficulties (see, for example, Luthar, Cicchetti and Becker 2000). Saleebey (2013) maintains that all environments, however bleak, have resources that can be used to develop resilience skills.

The Signs of Safety approach

The Signs of Safety approach accepts that risk assessment of violence defies accurate quantification. Telling a person what they ought *not* to do consists of nothing more than the absence of something, and we can rarely be sure that a behaviour has ceased. Neither does it help a person who is violent to work out how they will be different when they are non-violent. Instead, a Signs of Safety approach emphasises identifying existing signs of safety which are measurable and then develops these signs and expands them so that a safe-care plan can be put in place. The person is helped to do this but is held accountable for their behaviour in the future. Turnell and Edwards (1999) developed six practice principles in their Signs of Safety model:

- understanding the position of each family member

- finding exceptions to the violence

- discovering strengths and resources that can be used in the problem situation

- focusing on the goals of all involved people to ensure the safety of those most vulnerable

- scaling safety and progress

- assessing willingness, confidence and capacity to change.

We find that this structure is useful in working with all forms of violence as it recognises that safety is at the heart of the issue, and making the world less dangerous has to be a key element of any intervention. We hold strongly that people who have been violent should be given the opportunity to change and have found that this structure enables this to happen without compromising the safety of others. Indeed, our experience tells us that this approach helps to develop the resources and strengths of individuals and families in combating violence and moving toward a more productive future.

The rest of this book broadly follows the Signs of Safety structure and demonstrates how this is put into practice.

Chapter 2

Understanding the Position of Each Person

Respectfulness

Quite simply, respectfulness means treating the person with respect, regardless of the nature of the violence. An important component of respectfulness is resisting the temptation to (a) directly and forcefully challenge the person who has committed a violent act, and (b) demand that they admit fully their sinfulness, accept the impact of their behaviour on others and show remorse. In the first place, challenging a person about their behaviour is ineffective. Expecting someone to talk about their violent behaviour to a worker they have only just met ignores the fact that the person already knows that they have done something wrong but may well be feeling ashamed, embarrassed or fearful of the consequences of admitting their 'guilt'. These consequences commonly include potential losses to the person who has been violent: loss of a valued relative/friend's esteem, loss of freedom, loss of a job, loss of family and many more. The research shows that people tend to talk more openly and honestly about the violence once they have come to trust the worker. Thus, it is counterproductive to begin with direct confrontation as it will naturally meet resistance, which will be increased as each party continues to push their own story in an effort to be heard. Denial, resistance and mitigation are normal human responses to any perceived threat of loss.

PRACTICE ACTIVITY 2.1

Think of a time when taking full responsibility for an action would have had legal or financial consequences for you, such as a bump in your car, a lost piece of jewellery, accidental damage to a carpet.

- Were you able to accept full responsibility for your action, or did you deny or minimise events?

- What were the drivers for your responses?

(Bateman and Milner 2015, p.86)

Workers often believe that the person needs to be able to talk about their behaviour openly before they can 'move forward'. This is not only questionable, but impressing this notion upon people closes down the conversation they want to have with you. Carol sought counselling support after her ex-husband broke into her house and raped her. Of her counselling experience she said: 'I don't want to talk about it. It brings it all back and it's like it happening again and I come out crying and exhausted. I want to talk about how to get over it'.

PRACTICE ACTIVITY 2.2

Karen was struggling to care for her three young children when persistent harassment by neighbours escalated from verbal abuse to a lighted firework being pushed through her letterbox causing a significant fire. Her social worker is adamant that she talk about a time 8 years ago when she was the victim of a gang rape by strangers as she went to buy fish and chips. Karen can't see the relevance of this: 'It was years ago. I got over it quick because it wasn't like it was anyone I knew. They just picked on me because I was there. It could have been the next person to come by'.

- What do you think will be foremost on Karen's mind when you meet with her?

- How will you respond to her concerns, still keeping the children's welfare in mind?

At the other end of the violence spectrum, we find that people who have committed sexual violence are particularly reluctant to talk openly about what they have done. Daniel served a short prison sentence for the sexual abuse of his 15-year-old stepdaughter. Now in a new relationship, his baby boy has been taken into care while Daniel completes a sex offenders' assessment programme. He was puzzled how talking about his offending would make his baby safer and, being deeply ashamed of what he had done, said: 'It's going to be hard, but I'll tell my family and the psychologist. But him [the social worker] – he's the last person I want to talk to about it. I don't trust him. He's made up his mind that I'm just a bad person'. Interestingly, Daniel's elderly mother was very distressed on hearing his full confession; it had been enough for her to come to terms with the notion of her son being a sex offender without having to hear the sordid details. Did this constitute a therapeutic act of violence?

Second, it is surely not a good idea to treat those you hope will become more respectful to others with disrespect. Jenkins (1996) considers that trying to break down what you see as denial, minimisation and mitigation constitutes a therapeutic tyranny whereby the worker operates from a sense of self-righteous superiority, giving them a sense of entitlement, blame and vengeance. While the intention is to rectify the person's violent behaviour, it can all too easily be a demonstration of power differences. For example, on being informed that children were being bullied in his school, the head teacher responded with: 'Bullying? In *my* school!? I'll soon stamp that out'. The contradiction here is that he will deal with the problem of bullying by bullying. It also demonstrates the way we often talk about violence using negative – largely male – metaphors. These metaphors extend across the whole lifespan with violent people being sent to the naughty step when little, the sin bin or isolation as young people and being confronted and challenged about their behaviour when adult.

PRACTICE EXAMPLE 2.1

Four-year-old Oscar was a defiant child who responded to frustration with rage. He would throw whatever was at hand, kick doors and people, and race wildly about the house, endangering the physical safety of his baby brother. His parents were advised to put him on a naughty step but he curled into a tight ball behind the sofa when anyone tried to speak with him or lift him up. At other times he was a loving and charming boy who would promise to 'be good'.

A breakthrough came when his family moved house where the staircase had a wide square step on the bend. This was nominated the calm step and he was invited to go to it whenever he began to get angry. Oscar was happy to do this as there was room for him to curl up in the corner. In a short time, he was taking himself to the calm step without being asked to do so. His family learned to leave him in peace when he was on the calm step.

It is interesting to reflect that his hiding behind the sofa may not have been his way of escaping punishment, but his way of calming down.

PRACTICE ACTIVITY 2.3

It is quite common for people to ask the person to stop being violent and, like Oscar, they happily promise to cease the violence; however, this is a negative goal which is difficult to describe or measure.

- How would you help Oscar work out the details of 'being good' so that he knew what was expected of him?

- Think of a violent person with whom you are working and consider what that person would actively be doing differently when they become non-violent.

Couzens (1999) comments that it's hard to have an interesting conversation when everything is negative, but doing something about violence which involves serious harm to others is such an urgent concern that it often dominates the whole picture to the exclusion of all else. This has the effect of making that person feel worthless and unfairly judged.

PRACTICE EXAMPLE 2.2

Tony and Paige's arguments involved ash trays being thrown across the room and loud shouting. On one occasion Paige hit Tony on the head with a kettle, but as Tony had a history of fighting and was much stronger than Paige, he was viewed as dangerous, and their baby daughter was taken into care. Tony agreed to attend a violence-awareness course but was distressed at being accused of minimising his behaviour:

I've not had a serious conviction since 2008. No one takes that seriously. I have done stupid things in the past but I've turned it round. No one seems to think this is a good thing. They seem to concentrate on the bad things I've done.

When asked how he 'turned it round', Tony had no difficulty in talking openly about his history of fighting and how he had decided to leave fighting behind after being put on the vulnerable prisoners' wing.

Problem-free talk

One way of avoiding everything being negative is to engage in some problem-free talk. This is not to avoid the main issues but to help you find out what qualities the person has that can be used in safety building. Problem-free talk consists of asking about people's hopes, aspirations, hobbies and interests. This opens up a way of identifying tenderness. People may be quick to use their fists on other people but often reveal a tender side when they talk about their interests. Examples of tenderness we have discovered through asking about people's interests include:

- A man with a long history of physical violence over a series of situations and relationships had love and respect for his terriers.

- A seemingly out-of-control young person who bullied other pupils and attacked teachers was found to be caring and responsible when looking after his rabbits.

- A fighting girl who would smack anyone she suspected of disrespecting her was fiercely protective and tender with her disabled younger sister.

- An older woman whose impatience with workplace colleagues resulted in her getting a final warning for bullying turned out to have immense patience when grafting roses in her garden.

These qualities can all be grown on and developed to help the person work toward their preferred ways of being, and be of use in safety building. It's also helpful to ask the person what has happened between the violent behaviour and meeting with the worker. It's not uncommon for change to happen in this space, so it is important to start from there rather than the original incident.

PRACTICE ACTIVITY 2.4

The next time you meet with a person you are helping overcome their violence, explain that you've talked a lot about what has gone wrong, so now you would like to balance things up a bit and talk about what has gone well. Then ask questions such as:

- What was the best time you ever had?

- What is the hardest thing you have ever done?

- At what are you really good (slanted toward hobbies and interests)?
- If your pet could talk, what would it tell me about you?
- Any other helpful questions of which you can think.

We often demand retribution without realising that it can be another form of violence that reduces the scope for rehabilitation. For example, prisons are notoriously poor at preventing reoffending, and the conditions can be very brutal. Consider this statement from a prisoner:

> I'm locked in here because of my behaviour. My behaviour was not as reprehensible as that being meted out to me. Society condemns my behaviour but accepts the way I am treated. I don't understand this difference in standards and I can't accept it. I don't accept society's views on the treatment of inmates as I am experiencing it. I can't see how it improves anything as what remorse I may have felt has long since been replaced with anger and cynicism. (Hampton 1993, p.146)

Approaches that 'challenge' and 'confront' can be experienced by the person as bullying, insisting on change that is externally imposed rather than being encouraged from the person. This also replicates ideas of masculinity where, mainly male, perpetrators of violence are deemed to need aggressive approaches to 'break down' their beliefs and attitudes. We find that replicating male violence in therapeutic approaches is both ironic and ineffective.

Listening

If we don't challenge directly, what sort of conversations do we have instead? *Instead* is an important word in solution focused practice as it provides an opportunity to escape from stuck situations, interventions that are not working, stalemates and adversarial relationships to a fresh course of action. We do something differently, and that simple thing is listening to the violent person's perspectives and discovering how complex their lives are. This does not involve colluding with a mitigating account of violence; rather, it means listening respectfully to accounts of perceived unfairness, encouraging people to explore the meaning of their behaviour and the underpinning beliefs. For example, when we asked 13-year-old James how long fighting had been bothering him at school, he told us that he'd always been bad. He knew this because his family not only called him Dennis the Menace but actually bought him a red-and-black-striped jumper when he was 4 years old.

Listening respectfully enables people to move beyond superficial responses. For example, rather than challenging Geoff's description of a domestic-violence episode in which he accused his wife of being a prostitute, he was asked what he hoped to gain by calling her a prostitute, a question that invites him to elaborate on his beliefs about women or talk about his anger more generally. The conversation can then move on to consider the notion that, as we have control over our behaviour but not our feelings, it is all right to *feel* angry but not all right to *do* anger.

In listening to people's accounts, we strive to avoid categorising and labelling people. In the first place, the categorisation may well be wrong. Simon was being assessed following the discovery that he had filmed girls in the school showers. He complained bitterly about the results of his questionnaire:

> He (the psychologist) said I fitted the typical profile of a sex offender, but the questions were just like 'Do you drink a lot, sometimes or rarely?' and I answered them all in the middle. I don't see how he can tell anything from that? How is that going to help me?

In the second place, 'when a person is viewed as representative of a particular type of offender, the situational and complex variables that may be significant may be lost' (Lee *et al.* 2003, p.23).

PRACTICE ACTIVITY 2.5

Eileen freely admitted smacking her partner, Gemma, really hard several times. She agreed that what she had done was wrong but excused it to some extent by explaining that she was physically tired with taking on overtime when unwell in order to finance Gemma's fledgling business, which was still in the design stage. Rather than challenge this 'mitigation', her position in the relationship was explored. Listening to them talk about their hopes for the business and their future together, it emerged that Gemma was not only making heavy financial demands on Eileen but also excluding her from business developments. Gemma talked across Eileen, informing her that it couldn't be helped because they needed the money.

- Is there a clear victim here?

- What could you say to this couple that would enable their stories to be heard?

Building partnership

Turnell and Edwards say that when the worker understands and is responsive to the violent person's position, you have the first sign of safety: 'This openness is a key element in building cooperation, and it is the cooperative relationship that we see as the principle vehicle for creating change and increasing safety' (1999, p.57). This has the advantage of preventing the worker from getting stuck with a fixed theory about the violence and/or the person. Instead of translating what a person says to you into derogatory terms such as denial or resistance, the worker acknowledges how difficult it is to talk about what they have done. Jenkins (1990, p.66) suggests using questions that invite the person to talk constructively with the worker:

- It isn't easy – it takes a lot of courage to face up to the fact that you have hurt someone. How does it affect you to talk about your violence?

- Are you sure you can handle talking about what you have done?

- What does it say about you as a person that you are here today and telling me about what you have done?

Additional helpful questions are:

- What do you make of your current situation?

- From the report, you can see how others view things. What is your perspective on the situation?

- What is your theory about this?

- How do you explain this to other people?

- How would [the person who has been harmed] explain it?

- What effect has [the violence] had on your family/friends/work?

- Does it suit you to have this problem in your life?

- How has [the violence] changed things for your family/friends/work?

- What effect do you have on [the violence]?

- What would be helpful for you right now?

- Given a choice between [the violence] and life free of it, which do you choose?

- Suppose your life stays the way it is. What will change for you then?

- What options do you have when you are angry?

- Some people might say you need to do _____ in this situation. What do you think about that?

- I'm sure many people would say we're not interested in your opinions and what you want. Do you think that's true?

Talking with people who can't or won't talk

Although these questions usually engage people in partnership, there will always be the occasional person who really can't bring themselves to talk about their violent behaviour at all. We find this is most likely to occur where the behaviour feels particularly shameful; indeed, we heard of one young man actually falling asleep to avoid talking! We respect this position but ask questions that presume there will be a time when they can talk when we have understood their reluctance:

- What would help you feel more ready or able to talk about the behaviour?

- Are there some things you are happy to talk about now and other things we can talk about later?

- Can you tell me when 'talking' has been useful? What were the effects then?

- Who have you found to be the best person with whom to talk?

- Is there someone with whom you have already discussed the behaviour with whom I can talk, and then for us to meet after that?

- How about we plan today what we are going to discuss and then start the talking bit when we next meet?

- What does it say about you that you are ashamed of what you have done?

- What would it say about you if you were not ashamed?

(Adapted from Jenkins 2005a and 2005b)

Many people refuse to admit what they have done, even when there is overwhelming evidence to the contrary. While acknowledgement of responsibility is preferable, it is not a sign of safety as it doesn't hold the person accountable for change in the future (Turnell and Edwards 1999; Clark 2013). Questions which bypass this position include:

- What is more important to you, to be believed that you didn't do it or to get out of this mess?

- You say you are safe around [the person(s) harmed], so what is your hard evidence for this?

- What are you planning to do in the future to make sure that people can't make these allegations against you?

Where a child or young person is too embarrassed to talk or resentfully answering questions with monosyllables, we ask the child to change roles with the person who has come with them. This is usually a parent, but the technique would work equally well with a friend. The worker then interviews the pretend child while the real child is given two pieces of card on which are written CORRECT! and WRONG! to hold up after each answer. To help people stay in role, we begin by asking them to change seats and begin our questions in a deliberately serious tone of voice, prefaced by the child's name.

PRACTICE EXAMPLE 2.3

Darren's mum has brought him for help with his 'inability to control his temper' and 'communication difficulties'. The latter problem turns out to consist of not talking to adults at all, maintaining instead a sullen silence. Judith Milner addresses the problem.

Judith (to mum as Darren): Tell me, Darren, how long has this temper been in you?

Mum (as Darren): About 12 months. CORRECT!

Judith (to mum as Darren): So, Darren, is it worse or better at the moment?

Mum (as Darren): It's not as frequent. CORRECT!

Judith (to mum as Darren): Are the episodes as bad as previously?

Mum (forgetting her role as Darren): He's only had the one really bad one.

Darren has difficulty deciding which card to hold up, eventually proffering both.

Judith (to Darren): Is mum doing you well, Darren?

He nods.

Judith (to mum as Darren): What is the temper like?

Mum (as Darren): Like a volcano. Exploding. CORRECT!

Judith (to mum as Darren): Is it a slow or sudden volcano?

Mum (as Darren): Sudden. CORRECT!

Judith (to mum as Darren): What does it make you do?

Mum (as Darren): I don't know. (As herself): Here, Darren, you'll have to speak for yourself.

She changes places with him and takes the two cards.

Darren continues the conversation as himself with mum then starting to use the cards after he gives what she considers to be a WRONG! answer. They are both laughing and Darren is finding the conversation fun and non-threatening.

(For more details, see Milner 2001, pp.139–140.)

Although working with violence is a serious business (to appropriate Murray Parkes' (1972) comment on working with bereavement), that is no reason to take it solemnly. A little playfulness and the use of humour helps reduce tension and fearfulness which is often hidden by a front of bravado or sullenness. (For more ideas about playful ways of working with serious problems, see Freeman, Epston and Lobovits 1997 as well as Milner and Bateman 2011.)

Where a person persists with an inability to talk about what they have done, the Resolutions Approach developed by Essex and colleagues is helpful (Essex, Gumbleton and Luger 1996; Turnell and Essex 2006).

They devised a strategy whereby 'similar but different' stories are created that mirror the alleged harmful behaviour. This process:

- creates a context where parents can talk about the harmful behaviour without getting into denial stories and disputation (can't be used against them in court as it's not the real family)

- allows the non-abusing parent to consider other possibilities and strengthen the protective role

- creates a context where trust, responsibility, impact on children and so forth can be discussed in detail

- allows the exploration of difficult relational dynamics

- looks at people's perspectives, including the wider family.

PRACTICE EXAMPLE 2.4

Jackie has four children: Keira (age 10 years), Megan (age 8 years), Hope (age 7 years) and Maisie (age 4 years). Jackie and Keira have mild learning difficulties. Jackie's partner, Niall, is Maisie's father, although all the girls call him dad. He lives in a nearby town, preferring not to move in with Jackie on the grounds that she doesn't keep the house clean enough. Keira disclosed to her teacher that Niall had come into the girls' bedroom and put his hand under the covers, touching their private parts. Niall is only allowed to see Jackie and the girls outside both their homes. Niall persists in maintaining that he can't remember anything about the sexual touching and that, if it did happen – which he very much doubts – he must have been drunk. Despite the sexual touching, the girls want him back in their lives. Jackie too wants him back as the girls are easier to manage when he's around. After keep-safe work has been completed with the girls and Jackie has talked about her protective role, a 'similar but different' scenario is undertaken. The girls enter into the story with gusto, quickly choosing names for themselves (Lauren, Lucy, Holly and Honey, respectively) and practise what they will say to dad (Patrick) when he arrives with the family's social worker.

Despite Niall's persistence in denying the touching, as 'Patrick' he had no difficulty answering questions the girls wanted put to him and also safety-building questions such as those below:

- How do you think Lauren felt when she realised there was someone in the bedroom and that she was being touched on her private parts?

- How may she be feeling afterwards?

- How do you think this has affected the family?

- What do you think Patrick should say to Lauren?

- What first steps can he take to begin building safety in the home?

The girls added questions of their own, talking much more freely than they had in previous weeks about the impact of the touching and their feelings that they were responsible for breaking up the family. They were only really reassured that this was the right thing to have done when 'Patrick' said it was and that he shouldn't have gone into their bedroom and touched them. A safety plan was then developed from the themes and issues discussed. Afterwards, they all said how much easier it had been to talk in role rather than as themselves.

This case example is a fragment of what was a carefully planned and lengthy session. Before embarking on hypothetical-situation work with a family, the workers need to prepare all relevant family members and agree on roles between workers. We recommend reading Chapter 8 of Turnell and Essex (2006) as a preliminary step. (How safety plans are devised is explained in Chapters 3, 6 and 7.) Similarly, when working with a translator, it is important to meet with the translator beforehand and identify any words that may be difficult to translate literally, how to handle embarrassment, what confidentiality arrangements need to be made and so forth.

Do's for constructive conversations

The do's for constructive conversations are as follows:

- Be punctual, courteous, clean and tidy.

  This sounds self-evident, but we hear many complaints from people who have been violent about workers being late for sessions or meetings without apology, whereas any lateness on *their* part is ascribed to non-cooperation. We have also noticed in child protection conferences that the person who has done harm has dressed carefully for what they perceive as an important event, but many of the workers are scruffily attired. We also notice workers being rude; one woman coordinator of a child protection conference snapped at a father: 'Don't call me "love", my name is...'. Pressing a feminist point in a situation where the man is relatively powerless and the woman is relatively powerful is not merely inappropriate but constitutes a therapeutic tyranny.

- Take care that the place where you plan to talk with the person is appropriate.

  Many young children do not like being taken out of their classroom for a discussion of their behaviour. They worry about the questions that will be asked when they return to the classroom. Also, as buildings change function, they are not always suitable for adults who remember them from early contexts. Danny was expected to 'sit down with social workers in a non-confrontational manner and explore factors in his childhood that lead him to be violent'. The meetings were held in a Social Care office that previously had been the children's home where Danny experienced physical abuse (Milner 2008).

- Be available and accessible, with regular and predictable contact.

  One of a prisoner's 10 recommendations for workers is for more flexible arrangements (Denborough 1996, p.131). You may be constrained by agency arrangements in how frequently you can meet with a person, but you can remain accessible by inviting written and telephone contact. We find that flexibility actually reduces the number of sessions needed.

- Explain yourself and how you work.

  People need to know the purpose of your meeting with them, what the concerns are, what the options and choices are, details of any rules and boundaries – especially around confidentiality – and how long it will take.

- Check that the information you have is accurate.

  It often is not at all accurate, and even when it is, it may well be expressed in words and phrases the person finds offensive. This is particularly true of assessment reports which dwell wholly on the negative aspects of the behaviour and hint pessimistically that there is little hope without lengthy therapeutic intervention.

- Be curious.

  This helps you notice things which give a clue to solutions. For example, Alan and Natalie complained that they had difficulty in listening to each other without interrupting. Judith noticed that they listened to each other and talked calmly for over an hour on their first session for couples' fighting, even though they were a bit tense and upset. She was then able to be curious with them about how they did this.

- Only ask questions to which you do *not* know the answer.

  If you wait to hear the answer to your question before formulating what you say next, you will understand the position of the person more quickly: 'Understanding position is equivalent to understanding the plot in a play or story: once you get it, the characters and action make much more sense' (Turnell and Edwards 1999).

- Ask if you are asking relevant questions and if you have forgotten to ask anything that is important.

  Evaluating the interview is essential and need not be left until the end. This way you can avoid the stalemate of you trying to break down perceived resistance and the person resisting all the harder because they do not feel understood.

- Make your records and reports available to the person, using plain English and using that person's words as much as possible.

  Check the accuracy of your recording with them, asking, 'Have I got it right?'

Don'ts for constructive conversations

The don'ts for constructive conversations are as follows:

- Don't label people.

  It's not helpful to think you know what this person is like and why they are like that until you have sought to understand them. They may well surprise you.

- Don't trivialise their concerns about unfairness in their lives as minimising.

  Unfairness is not an excuse for violence, but it *is* a part of the person's life that needs to be acknowledged. Ian had played an active part in Northern Ireland during the troubles, where he had gained a reputation as a hard man. On listening to his explanation of his position, Ian talked about how his moving away to try to build a life free of the reputation as being a 'hard man' was as much a burden as an advantage. He was aware of how his experiences had brutalised him and he was keen to discover ways of being different.

- Don't come up with solutions.

  Ignore theoretical explanations for violence and concentrate on understanding the person without the labels and possible causes. That person's own solution will be best because the person will claim it and commit to it.

- Don't interpret what they are saying in terms of your favourite theory.

  Take what they are saying at face value and, if you don't understand what they are saying, ask respectful questions.

- Don't edit what they tell you when you write your notes of the meeting or prepare your report.

  A looked-after teenager who had been in secure accommodation twice as a result of her violent behaviour had three psychiatric reports attached to her referral form – and three different psychiatric diagnoses. When asked how she would diagnose herself, she replied simply: 'When I don't have the support I need, I fuck up'. This is a perfectly suitable problem definition from which to start work on a possible solution.

- Don't ask why.

  It's a blaming question and doesn't take you anywhere.

Once position is understood, the worker must consider how to use this knowledge in the search for a solution. The next step in this process is addressed in the next chapter, but although we offer a framework for working with violence, it is not necessarily a sequence. The different elements can overlap, and understanding the position of the person will continue as the work progresses – and that position will change and develop too.

Chapter 3

Finding Exceptions or Unique Outcomes to Violence and Conflict

PRACTICE EXAMPLE 3.1

After being caught on camera on five occasions over the Christmas period shoplifting in Tesco, the television chef Antony Worrall Thompson, expressed remorse and puzzlement, saying he felt immense shame over his behaviour, which he was at a loss to explain, and that he was seeking help from a psychoanalyst.

Clearly Mr Worrall Thompson is expecting lengthy problem-searching sessions with his psychoanalyst. Should he meet with a solution focused worker, his experience would be markedly different to his expectations. Rather than asking questions about the problem, the solution focused worker searches for *exceptions* to the problem, those times when the problem might reasonably have been expected to happen but didn't. This implies that safe behaviour was present, if only for a fleeting moment, so Mr Worrall Thompson would simply be asked, 'Tell me about the times when you could have shoplifted but didn't do so'. His childhood experiences of abuse may or may not be relevant to why he stole from Tesco but, either way, it would be important to develop a solution that prevents him from shoplifting in the future.

de Shazer (1991) argues logically that there are always exceptions; otherwise, the person wouldn't know they had a problem. For example, how would you know you were depressed if there was no variation in how you felt? There is nothing that happens *always* in human relationships; no one loses their temper with everyone all the time; no couple are always in conflict. But if the exceptions which contain the seeds of solutions are not asked about, they can go unnoticed.

PRACTICE ACTIVITY 3.1

Think of a small problem you have been experiencing.

- When has the problem been less of a problem?

- What was happening when the problem was less?

- What were you doing when the problem was less?

- How did you do this?

- How can you do more of it?

(Myers 2007, p.19)

The occasions when the person was frustrated and angry but was not violent are examined in detail to discover where, when and how it occurred, what was different, how this is understood, and if they can do more of it – what Turnell and Edwards (1999) call discovering the '95%' of behaviour which is non-violent rather than focusing on the '5%' of problematic behaviour. As well as asking the person who has harmed someone about exceptions, Turnell and Edwards recommend that you also ask those who complain about the person's violence for exceptions. To get your attention and intervention, the referrer is highly likely to emphasise the problem even when there is evidence of safe behaviours as well. The more the problem is talked about, especially in meetings, the bigger it gets so that everyone can end up worrying about the risk the person poses rather than seeking to develop safety. Risk is difficult to quantify as high-risk people don't always reoffend and low-risk people sometimes do. However, safety is quantifiable and measurable, so it is vital to identify every small or large sign of it.

Persistence is required in the search for exceptions. It may be that there are no current exceptions; for example, in some contested contact cases, divorced parents may be locked in conflict but there will be historical exceptions. The exceptions can be very small and only tangential to the relationship; for example, Jack could only think of one exception when he wanted to hit someone but didn't: 'My brother...last night, he wound me up and I wanted to smack him.

I said, "Shut up, you're winding me up" and walked out'. When asked how he did that, he replied, 'Well, it weren't my flat and I didn't want to get blood on the walls. If it'd been my own flat, I'd have hit him'. Although miniscule in terms of temper control, it was an important exception from which to begin building responsibility-taking because it had meaning to his life. Domestic-violence offenders regularly complain of not being able to respond to probation officers using hypothetical situations in their discussions on the grounds that these situations lack reality for them: 'She asked what would I do if someone came up to me at the bus stop and hit me. I said I'd deck him. She said I should walk away from it. She's always asking me daft things like that. She says I'm past helping'.

When exceptions are found, we examine them in detail asking questions related to how, where, when and what else. Asking the person how they did the exception is important as it begins talk about how the person does the solution. It shifts control and responsibility to the person, creating stories that make it possible to learn from what is already there and to see success. Asking detailed questions about exceptions identifies skills and competencies that can be built upon in solution finding. Exception-finding questions include:

- When are you not...?

- When are you less...?

- When you feel like that and you don't do it, what do you do instead?

- How did you do that?

- What will it be like when [the exception] is happening more?

- Who will notice when it is happening more?

- Who could help you do [the exception] more?

Having identified exceptions, it is important for the worker to resist praising the person's efforts. It is tempting to say 'well done', but such a response has two effects: first, it closes down that phase of the conversation, potentially causing you to miss more exceptions. Second, it establishes you as the person with the expertise to praise, which they may dismiss – or come to need. Instead, we aim to assist the person in praising themselves as this helps them recognise their safe behaviours. We do this by offering indirect compliments such as, 'So you could have hit out, but you didn't. What does that say about you as a person?' Or 'Did you know that about yourself?' Similarly, 'noticing' is more effective in increasing safety than praise, especially with children who exhibit defiant as well as aggressive behaviour. Indeed, lavishly praising children lets them know exactly what to do the next time they want to annoy you – the opposite of what was praised.

It is not unusual to get a 'don't know' reply to exception-finding questions. This is partly because it is not something the person had thought about before, the talk being mainly about the problem, and partly because people expect the worker to supply the answers. We expect people to work out their own solutions, so we take the view that if they did it (the exception), we are quietly confident that they do know how they did it but just don't realise it *yet*. Therefore, we slow down and give them time to think. There are questions you can ask to shift the expertise from you to the person in this situation:

- No reaction, other than a puzzled expression (after all it is their turn to speak).

- Maybe you know and don't know at the same time – that's hard to say...

- Acknowledge they 'don't know' and wait, pretending that's not the answer.

- I always think when people do things they must have some idea how to do it...

- Of course you don't know yet; so what do you think?

- Okay, so what do you think your mum/partner/best friend would know?

- Suppose you did know, what might the answer be?

- Guess.

- Perhaps I've not asked this question in a helpful way – how could I ask it better?

- [For small children] Oh I see. It's a secret. Okay.

- Perhaps you might like to study what happens next time that happens and see if you can spot how you do it?

(Milner and O'Byrne 2002, p.43)

A question we use a lot when searching for exceptions and enlarging on them is 'What else?' There almost always is 'something else' if you go slowly enough and persistently ask for more details. People just aren't used to talking about what they have done well, which means that exception stories lack the weight and density of problem stories, so we need to thicken the new, budding solution, what narrative therapy calls the 'counterplot'. One way of doing this is to spell out the exceptions in feedback notes. We will describe different ways of recording safety plans later, but below is an example of feedback notes using a framework devised by Berg and Reuss (1998). This is a useful framework as it allows for the exceptions – *what* the person did – to be separated from *how* they did it, using their own words. Knowing how one did something gives a person confidence that they can do it again.

PRACTICE EXAMPLE 3.2

This couple were in danger of having their children taken into care unless they could cease fighting.

Problem

Kylie and Troy had difficult lives when they were younger, and things are not so easy now that they are living unsupported with three young children. They are shut in with each other all the time and this leads to fighting and upset. Fighting in front of the kids doesn't help improve the kids' behaviour.

Kylie and Troy would like to get back to enjoying themselves again. They have a lot of love for each other and have been together for nearly 10 years.

Exceptions and progress

- Troy used to hit back when Kylie fought with him, but he has stopped doing this.

- Troy used to annoy Kylie by keeping things bottled up, but he is now more able to talk about things that upset him. He is more open with Kylie and this helps them tell each other what they are thinking and what they need.

- Even though Kylie fights and breaks up Troy's things sometimes, she has never used put-downs when they argue about silly little things.

- They are not as violent as they thought they were. When they answered questions on the 'overcoming violence' chart (see Appendix), it turned out that they can both accept that the other person has a right to be upset, they respect each other's opinions, they can be honest without fear, they take responsibility for any harm done, they know it is not right to use violence to get their own way, they can control their drinking and they plan to promote a violence-free relationship.

- They have only had one argument in the past three months. This one lasted only a couple of hours and they were both able to calm down and sort it out.

- They didn't have any arguments before all the children arrived and they were not so tired.

Solutions

- Troy stopped hitting back by giving in, that is, backing off arguments.

- Troy was able to talk about bad things in his earlier life with their social worker and can now tell Kylie when he needs help. This helps Kylie calm down.

- Kylie doesn't use put-downs because she is considerate of Troy's feelings.

- Despite that the arguments over silly little things get out of hand at times, Kylie and Troy are still able to love and respect each other. They are also willing to work on getting things better.

- They handled the last argument differently: Kylie went to bed and Troy considered sleeping downstairs (like they usually do in the middle of an argument), but he decided to go upstairs with a cup of tea for Kylie. She bit her tongue when he came up. The argument did not occur. They are proud of themselves for this. As Kylie says, it is a big milestone that they have overcome this.

- Tiredness is a big problem as they fall into bed as soon as the children are settled. Weekends are not good either. They plan to change this.

Next steps

They intend to brainstorm a blueprint for the changes they need to make in their lives so that their tenth wedding anniversary will be a celebration of things going smoothly. These changes might be Troy training for a different job, it might be Kylie going to work, it might be sharing the housework – or it might be something completely different. Whatever the case, it will include a lot of cherishing as Kylie hopes to retake her vows when they get to 10 years.

Separating the person from the problem

Where people find it hard to talk about their harmful behaviour at all, it is helpful to externalise the problem. This is especially the case with people who have been sexually harmful, couples in bitter post-divorce conflict situations and children who have been much criticised. Some problems have so much weight that they silence and immobilise people. It is difficult for people to change when the problem has become an integral part of their character and they become their labels – delinquent, defiant, dangerous and so forth. Problem-saturated stories limit people, especially when the prescribed 'expert' solution fails to work. Many people become defeated and depressed by their problem selves. In these instances it is useful to separate the person from the problem via *externalising* conversations (White and Epston 1990; White 1995). Talking about the problem as separate from the person relieves the pressures of blame, defensiveness and failure, freeing up the person – and significant others – to have a different relationship with the problem, one in which they can all gang up on the *problem* rather than the person.

A simple way of externalising the problem is to decide upon a name for it, one that reflects its unique qualities, and identify parts of it that are affecting everyone. For example, young people who have been sexually harmful tend to choose problem names such as The Touching Problem or Doing Sexy Things, while angry and aggressive children choose names such as Red Devil, Trouble or Fireball. Children frequently like to draw their named problem. Adults are not usually as imaginative as children and young people, usually naming their problem as Red Mist or Conflict, although the problem name does develop as externalising conversations grow. For example, one man who served a prison sentence for throwing his wife down the stairs and then stamping on her named his problem as Twaddling On after identifying the onset of his violent outbursts.

The problem is examined in great detail to discover its individual characteristics, for example, anger or temper or frustration – and then talked about as an enemy that is residing within the person. Externalising questions include:

- Where does Temper reside; for example, does it start with thoughts in the head or churning in the stomach?

- What does Frustration get you to do?

- Does it suit you to be dominated by Conflict?

- Conflict has a grip on you. How did it get its claws into you so much?

- How can you shake Conflict off?

- Can you think of times when you have resisted the invitations of The Touching Problem?

- Does it suit you to be pushed around by the Red Devil?

The aim of externalisation is not just to separate the person from the problem but also develop a sense of incongruence between the two, so the complained-about person becomes an active participant in the plan to beat the problem. This leads to conversations about where to put the problem. With a couple who brought High Conflict to a divorce-mediation session, matters were prevented from escalating further by asking them to consider leaving 'High Conflict outside the door for the rest of the session – make it wait there – it's stopping you from what you need to do' (Milner and O'Byrne 2002, p.111). Similarly, a 5-year-old boy disconnected from being a 'bad boy' by naming his problem Trouble and leaving it in the fridge when he went to school (Denborough 1996, p.101).

Externalising is of particular importance when working with people who have been harmed by violence as they often internalise the harm, blaming themselves. Choosing to disconnect from the disabling after-effects – deciding to discard intrusive thoughts, nightmares, self-blame and so forth by naming them and then disposing of them – enables people to reclaim their selfhood and move away from victimhood. For example, one young woman would shower in cold water to wash

The Dirt off her and watch it going down the plug hole. Then she would relax in a warm bath. Others prefer to dispose of the problem in a more physical way, for example, choosing to throw a written account over a cliff. (For more details on externalising abuse stories, see Chapter 3 in Milner 2001.)

PRACTICE EXAMPLE 3.3

Mark is a 12-year-old boy with learning difficulties. His mother complains that he steals, lies, kicks, bites, spits and has temper tantrums. She said, 'Either he goes into care or I'll put him six feet under. His dad won't be in the same room as him and his sisters are not speaking to him'. She was very dubious about him changing his behaviour as 'he can't concentrate for more than a few minutes'. This is a problem-saturated story, so his mother was asked for any exceptions to his bad behaviour. She listed: doing jobs for people, being a bit helpful, being a bit kind, being good with his hands, being very creative, being very imaginative and always being on the go. Judith said she was going to describe Mark and he must correct her if she gets him wrong: 'You sound like a specially talented person who has two parts. Does Frustration perhaps turn the talented person into the badly behaved one?' Mark seized on this explanation, which separated him from the problem, but explained that it was Temper rather than Frustration, and that is was red, like a bomb exploding, and that he had no control over it.

Finding exceptions

Judith: How long has the Red Temper been stopping you from being a good person?

Mark: Seven years.

Judith: Have you ever beaten it?

Mark: Yes. At my old school. I was good for 5 weeks. I got this sticker book and some sweets.

Judith: Can you remember how you did it?

Mark: No.

Judith: Can mum remember?

Mum: No. Just one day he came home with a good behaviour award and was over the moon. I said keep it up and he did till something snapped, and then he went backward.

Judith: Can you remember any other times he beat the temper?

Mum: Yes. He was good over the holidays when he could play out, but I don't like the ones he mixes with. He's got loads of energy.

Mark offered to make a cup of tea at this point; the offer was accepted, and then Red Temper was examined in more detail to find more exceptions. He worked out that he got up with Red Temper and clumped downstairs, and it would help if mum reminded him to get his things ready the night before.

Despite the externalising conversation, Mark still wasn't sure how he did good behaviour, but he did feel confident that he could do *more* good behaviour. It was likely also that the conversation would help his mum spot good behaviour and help him work out how he did it.

Mark gained control of his temper very quickly, with only four sessions being needed of which two were to strengthen the 'counterplot'. Knowing how to do the required behaviour and talking about this is much more productive than analysing bad behaviour.

(For more details, see Milner 2001, pp.29–31.)

Additional helpful questions are as follows:

- What name do you give to your problem?

- How would you draw your problem?

- When does [the problem] not trouble you or trouble you less? What is different at those times?

- How would you notice if you had more control of [the problem]?

(For many more questions, see Bannink 2006.)

Where exceptions are relevant to the problem

People will often claim to have little or no control over their violence, but asking for exceptions surprises them. For example, Vicky never hit her husband in front of the children; Nadir lost his temper at home and in the car, but never at work. Both people would not see these exceptions as relevant to the problem in the first instance as they would be thinking about the situational variables, but talking about them invites the person to begin taking responsibility for their loss of control.

PRACTICE ACTIVITY 3.2

- What questions would you ask Vicky that would start her thinking about how she was able to maintain self-control when she is with her children?

- How would you relate this to her current situation?

- Would your questions to Nadir be similar or different?

PRACTICE ACTIVITY 3.3

Amber is in danger of having her children taken into care following complaints from her partner, Peter, that she beats him up in front of them. She tells you that she has a nasty temper and she would love to be able to control it, as it gets in the way of being allowed to be a good mother. She describes her temper as red, *bright* red. All she can see is red. It starts in her eyes. Sometimes it comes suddenly, other times it builds up more slowly. She gets hot all over when it starts and annoyed that she can't control it. This makes it worse. Being hot goes to her eyes and she gets hot tears. It builds and builds until she feels like she is mad, and there is no way out of it. Then she lashes out with her fists, throws things (anything) and then her mouth starts and she shouts and screams (using foul language). It can last for days and then she feels worse afterwards – thinks *What the hell have I done?* Mostly Peter gets hit.

The temper moved in with Amber 12 years ago, after she was abused. This means that sometimes she gets angry toward herself. She feels like a doormat with everyone; even Peter expects her to do a lot for him, he puts her down and he doesn't give much back. She would like to stop being a doormat and control the temper instead of *it* controlling her.

She identifies several exceptions to the temper controlling her:

- The temper only builds up when Peter tells her she's a bad mother; other times, it is only a lighter red. Looking at the kids smiling always calms Amber down and stops the temper building up to the bright red colour. She can pull the temper back these times.

- Amber used to reach for things when the temper built up, but she doesn't do this any more. She stopped reaching for things after she got a warning from the police and was locked up for a short while.

- The temper mostly winds her up when she is with Peter. She can back it down other times by laughing at it and walking away. This makes her feel good.

- She can be good to herself and less of a doormat when the temper is not there. Then she is smiling and feels good about herself. She has feelings for Peter, but the love has gone and she feels better about herself without him there.

How can these exceptions be used to build safety?

What questions might you want to ask Peter?

Where the exceptions don't seem relevant

Frequently exceptions are reported that don't seem at all relevant to the situation under discussion. Some people hold others responsible for their violence: 'If she didn't wind me up, I'd be okay'. Other people deny any responsibility for the exceptions: 'It just happened; I didn't do anything'. Or in the case of bitter divorce disputes: 'Everything would be all right if he just disappeared'. However, exceptions can usually be found with persistent curiosity. Fifteen-year-old William dismissed the time he could have abused a young boy but didn't due to circumstances outside his control – his friend was in the next bedroom and he was afraid of being caught – but persistent curiosity about *what else* was happening revealed that he had built up an emotional attachment to this boy and that lessened his sexual feelings. (For more details, see Bateman and Milner 2015, pp.35–37.) Despite having hit his girlfriend, Hamad didn't see himself as a violent person: 'We all have a temper line we can step over or hold back' – so he was asked about times he was able to 'hold back'. He replied that he would like to be approachable and cool headed, but he gets anxious all the time and then he explodes. Searching for exceptions to anxiety became the starting point for building safety. Asking questions about safety and tenderness often reveals exceptions to the violent behaviour.

PRACTICE EXAMPLE 3.4

Although only in her early fifties, Lena's physical health is poor following a stroke. She has recently been diagnosed with diabetes and is currently in hospital following a fall. She has a black eye and nursing staff are concerned that she is being injured by her teenage son, Damian. Both Lena and Damian deny this is the case, but Lena has previously complained to neighbours that he pushes and hits her. (Damian is living with Lena because he was evicted from his flat due to being in arrears with the rent.)

Damian did say that his mother needed a lot of care and could be demanding. The stresses and frustrations involved in being a teenage carer for his mother, but also dependent on her for accommodation, were acknowledged – understanding the position of the person. Damian was then asked how he rated his mother's safety, how she could be safer and what he could do to make her safer. Acknowledging his difficulties and talking about his future behaviour enabled Damian to talk freely about the times he had coped with his mother's demands and how he could cope better.

Some people's lives are so saturated with violence that it is necessary to seek exceptions in many different scenarios. For example, Danny didn't want to give up violence altogether. As he explained, being a retired drug dealer was a dangerous position to be in; once people knew he was no longer dealing, they would have no fear of him and he would lay himself open to old scores being settled. He needed to continue giving people 'the eye' on the streets – but not in conversations with social workers. Equally, his partner did, indeed, wind him up. She said of the beating he gave her, 'I didn't deserve it, but I did ask for it. I wound him up' (Milner 2008). Danny's usable exception lay in a situation where he felt confident and safe: he never lost his temper with his children. Asking him how, where and when he kept his temper with the children when they were being difficult enabled Danny to work out how he was capable of being calm, quiet and patient despite being in a testing situation.

Similarly, Jack's life was saturated in violence. His problem was that he had hit his wife and he wanted control over his temper so she would take him back, but his violence was encouraged in other situations; neighbours sent for him to 'sort out' any trouble on the street, his employers gave him jobs in districts where he needed to be a tough man and – like Danny – if he lost his reputation for toughness, he would leave himself vulnerable to attacks:

Jack: Andy (his flat mate) and his brothers got into a fight in a pub and t'youngest got glassed and he's got to have a total facial reconstruction. Andy and his brothers are always getting beaten up because they are thickos. I saw father of t'lads what did it coming up t'road with four lads. I said, your lads been at it again, dishing it out. He started gobbing and picked a bottle up. I got out of t'van and hit him.

Judith: Hitting him, could you have handled that differently?

Jack: No. He were coming at me with a bottle. I was telling him calm and I only punched him once. Knocked him to floor and then got back in van.

Judith: Can you think of a time recently when you felt like punching someone but you didn't?

Jack: I looked out of t'flat winnder and saw me car mirror were hanging off. I went down and this chap were staggering on t'road. I asked him if he'd done it, and he offered to pay for it. He were drunk so I followed him on t'road to see if t'address he'd given me were t'right one. He turns into t'house and I knocked on 'door and this woman came out. I said 'Is that your husband? he's just knocked me wing mirror off'. She said, 'He's just come back from t'pub in a taxi. Gave me a mouthful and shut door. I brayed [banged] on t'door and she gave me another mouthful. I asked to see her husband. He come down and admitted it so I said I'd get it done cheap like. He come round next day and apologised and paid. I didn't rob him. Got one second hand. I handled that okay, including his wife. Before, I'd've kicked door in. I didn't give her a mouthful back or nowt like that.

We are confident that with patience, persistence and understanding the position of the person, it is possible to develop exceptions which do not seem obviously relevant to the problem into usable safety planning. We do, however, admit to one occasion when we found an exception we couldn't use (see below).

PRACTICE ACTIVITY 3.4

Having made great progress in controlling his violence, Jack was reconciled with his wife, but they were still living apart as a trial period. He saw her sister as the biggest stumbling block to his being allowed back into the family home, reporting that she was telling lies about him and that she had come up to him at a family barbecue and hit him in the face with a beer glass for no reason. On being asked if he could remember a time when he was getting on with his sister-in-law, he replied, 'Yes, when I was shagging (i.e. having sex with) her'.

• What is your next question for Jack?

Where there are no exceptions at all

In this situation you can ask the person to do a prediction task: ask the person to predict how they are going to be on any given day and see if their predictions are accurate. If they are accurate, then there are exceptions to be found; however, the absence of exceptions means there are no clear protective factors and therefore no safety. The vulnerable people in this situation are in danger and need external protection.

PRACTICE EXAMPLE 3.5

Henry developed a belief that his wife, Jane, was having an affair because of her leg movements in bed when sleeping. He was convinced this indicated an orgasm so, frustrated by vehement denials, he verbally abused the local vicar and then burst into Jane's workplace and hit her employer. Neither man reported the attack to the police. Henry was asked about times when he resisted his strong feelings of sexual jealousy. There were none; indeed, when asked about their early relationship, he replied that he'd had his doubts about her then. So despite Jane's hopes for a solution, she was offered a refuge place while psychiatric help was sought. The psychiatric service did not consider him dangerous enough for compulsory hospitalisation and he refused voluntary help, so his adult daughters were contacted and they supported their mother in leaving him.

Recording signs of safety

Turnell and Edwards (1999) devised a comprehensive safety assessment process that documents both concerns and safety alongside identifying the goals and perspectives of both professionals and family members. The primary focus is on developing and increasing levels of safety for children; thus, parents are required to demonstrate behaviour that is measurably safe. The assessment is structured so that parents understand others' concerns and what needs to be different for the professionals to be no longer concerned – outcomes for the children. What is already happening that contributes to child safety is acknowledged and used as a basis for increasing safety in other areas of family life. This process can also be used in assessments in other settings where there are vulnerable people. For example, an initial safety assessment of Henry's situation would look something like that shown in Table 3.1.

Table 3.1 Example of an initial safety assessment of Henry's situation

Concerns	Evidence of safety	What safety will look like
Henry has been physically and verbally violent toward people.	Jane is currently in a refuge and leaving Henry.	Henry will be non-violent toward Jane and others.
Henry believes that his wife is having an affair and does not believe her denials.		
There are concerns that Henry will be violent toward his wife.		Jane will feel safe.
Henry has always had strong feelings of sexual jealousy and there are no current exceptions to this.	Their daughters are acting in a supportive and safety-oriented way.	
Henry has refused psychiatric help.		Henry will accept that his sexual jealousy is irrational.
Psychiatric help cannot be mandated for Henry.		

In terms of goals, (a) Henry's goals are not yet clear, (b) Jane would like a solution to their current relationship problems and (c) the agency wants Jane to be safe and Henry to accept psychiatric help.

PRACTICE ACTIVITY 3.5

Lincoln is living apart from his children following an assault on his daughter, Milly, the third of his eight children (aged 13 years to 18 months) with Lily. He has regular, supervised contact with his children. He is permitted to phone Lily. He has no contact with Dee, the mother of his 15-year-old son, Sam. Table 3.2a indicates the progress he has made, all but one item of which is in the middle column. He is making progress, but it is early in the process.

Decide what measurable indicators of safety Lincoln needs to demonstrate (in relation to the four professionals' goals for Lincoln given in Table 3.2b) for you to be happy for him to return to the family home.

Table 3.2a Second safety assessment: Sam, Dane, Sean, Milly, Megan and Mark

Concerns (historic and recent)	Progress	Safety
Lincoln hit Dee's head against a wall when she was holding Sam when he was a baby (historic).		
He has been violent to Lily, witnessed by Dane and Sean (historic).		
Dane and Sean report being afraid of Lincoln when he is 'in a mood' after drinking cider and smoking cannabis (historic).		Since leaving the family home, all Lincoln's drink and drug tests have been negative.
He had heated arguments with Lily, witnessed by the children (recent).	He is talking calmly on the phone with Lily.	
	He is handling his frustration at the separation calmly.	
Milly, Megan and Mark are scared when their dad shouts, becomes angry and throws things (recent).	On contact Mark told his dad that his face was stern, and Lincoln apologised.	
	He has been keeping his voice quiet on contact, explaining things to the children, and working on temper control with the older children.	

Concerns (historic and recent)	Progress	Safety
He hit Milly when she disrespected him (recent).	When Milly did a pretend disrespect (a fake tongue ring), Lincoln stayed calm and controlled his upset.	
	He allows the children to disagree with him, and gives explanations.	
	He asks the children what they have been doing and praises them.	
	The older children say that he is doing discipline without shouting.	
	He gives all the children attention and talks to them one at a time.	
	He plays with the little ones at their own level (e.g. in the playhouse, reading stories).	
	All the children greet him enthusiastically and say how much they are enjoying seeing him.	
	Lincoln is less tense about being supervised and is enjoying the children too.	

Table 3.2b Goals of everyone involved

Children's goals	Lincoln's goals	Professionals' goals
Have dad back home and no shouting.	Show Lily his love for her and be a good father to his children.	Have more conversations with the children, praise them and enjoy them.
		Do discipline without shouting.
		Understand the impact of the assault on Milly.

All the family to show more respect for each other.	Talk quietly and calmly, praise the children and talk to them all, one at a time.	Safety for Lily.

PRACTICE ACTIVITY 3.6

Below are the notes from a session with Konika. Convert these notes into chart form, listing the concerns and goals.

Session notes

Name: Konika

Problem

Konika has been having a dreadful time at her home where she is racially harassed by one man in particular. After she got arrested and held overnight for threatening this man, her teenage children, Marley and Jennifer, were accommodated in foster care and then made the subject of an interim care order. Konika has been involved with Social Care for a long time and the court wanted to know how she will manage her emotional responses when stressed so that the children are not affected by them, and how she will be able to work with the professionals who are trying to help her so that the children can be returned to her care.

Konika wants this element out of her life so that she can move to another address near the city centre; get Social Care out of her life; get back on her information technology (IT) course; and to bring out a comic for people from ethnic minorities. To get this element out of her life, she will need to get her tipping point with frustration higher (it's at about 5–6 at the moment). Then she will be able to stay in her next house; be calm and peaceful; have good relationships with the teachers of Marley and Jennifer; the kids will be attending school regularly; and she will be on cordial terms with her neighbours and have community support.

Progress

- Konika can live peacefully with her neighbours. She was doing this before the racial harassment started.

- She can sometimes handle frustration and get her tipping point up a bit.

- Konika does know about her body language, even if she doesn't always do anything to alter it.

- She has lots of good qualities that she can use to handle stress and get her tipping point up by looking at her actions and how they affect her children.

Solutions

- How Konika does living peacefully with her neighbours is by keeping to herself mostly but being polite and saying hello and good morning, and going to events when invited.

- She handles frustration when she recognises it coming – her body language changes and she gets tense and turns away. She can feel the adrenalin surge and this makes her anxious, so she gets up and goes before she gets louder vocally. She did this in the supermarket when a woman accused her of dropping a tin can. She walked off calmly. This worked for her – but didn't get the shopping done! Music and tidying up in the garden help with stress relief too.

- Konika learned about body language from her psychiatrist. He explained that tall people can be intimidating and that going into a meeting hostile means that she's non-communicating and not going to get her point across. She also knows how to be appropriately assertive when faced with racial harassment; she would say she's proud to be of African descent, be confident and not shout back because it's only jealousy.

- The good qualities Konika has are intelligence (she found this out when she did her IT course), her sense of humour, loyalty to friends, dependability and love of her children, which keeps her focused. Her social worker says that she also is lively and fun.

Conclusion

Exception finding marks the beginning of the solution-finding phase of the interview, so it is helpful to mark this by saying something like: 'We've talked a lot about the problem; therefore, is it okay if I ask you some different sorts of questions now?' People expect workers to talk about the problem and give advice – even when they don't want to talk and have no intention of accepting any advice – so it is important to persist with solution focused talk. Turnell and Edwards (1999) recommend that you ask an exception question slightly differently three times before you decide there is no answer. Remember also to ask 'What else?' three times and say 'Instead of…' lots of times.

Chapter 4

Setting Achievable Goals

Defining goals

It is important to have clear goals, as otherwise you will have no way of knowing whether or not your work has been effective. Goals need to be measurable, achievable and ethical. A simple way of doing this is by asking everyone in the situation:

- How will you know that meeting with me will be worthwhile?

- What will you notice?

- What are your best hopes?

- What will need to happen for you to know that our work is helpful to you?

- What will other people notice?

When working with violence the focus is on the goals of *all* involved people to ensure the safety of those most vulnerable. These goals are set through negotiation with all parties and, rather than accepting a blanket goal of the violence stopping, what will be happening differently when all parties consider that safety and well-being is present are identified. This is rarely a straightforward process as people often disagree about what a good outcome would be; for example, it is not unusual in domestic-violence cases for social workers to want the parents to separate, whereas the parents want to stay together but for the violence to stop. This leads to parents agreeing to separate in order to keep their children but continuing to see each other. When found out, they are then accused of non-compliance with the 'contract', although it was actually never negotiated. Teachers often express a simple goal: for the young person to be removed to another place.

This will keep one set of pupils safe, but what about everyone else? Liam, a 14-year-old white boy with mild learning difficulties, had been excluded from school for fighting and using racial language. The exclusion increased his resentment as his fighting and verbal abuse had been in response to taunts from Asian pupils (the school population was 90% Asian). Liam reacted by racially abusing Asian shopkeepers, simply shifting his problem behaviour to another setting. Parents' goal for their children's aggression is, as we saw in the examples of Oscar and Darren in Chapter 2, for their child to be good or taken into care. As we have mentioned previously, 'being good' is an ill-defined goal. What does 'goodness' look like? How would you measure it?

PRACTICE ACTIVITY 4.1

Workers' goal are all too often very vague, for example, 'She will understand why she feels the need to engage in fights' or 'He will recognise the impact his behaviour has on others'.

- What difference will it make in terms of future behaviour if these goals are met?
- How would you measure the outcome?

One father whose baby had been removed from his care on discovery that the man has a teenage history of sexual harm complained, 'It's like they've kidnapped my kid but they won't tell me what the ransom is'. Similarly, workers sometimes confuse inputs and outputs with outcomes: providing an anger management course is an input, attending it is an output, and a person changing their behaviour as a result of attending the course is an outcome. We have heard many complaints from people that they have done everything asked of them, such as *attending* enhanced thinking, alcohol awareness and victim-empathy courses, but still have not satisfied the worker as their behaviour hasn't changed. The outcomes the worker expects to result from attendance at courses need to be spelled out in behavioural terms. Furthermore, sometimes there is a difference in goals due to different professional viewpoints; for example, a mental health service may want looked-after children returned to their mother to relieve her depression, whereas the child care service would have a different focus.

PRACTICE ACTIVITY 4.2

Think of a person with whom you are working but not making as much progress as you would like.

- List your goals for the work.

- Ask that person what *their* goals are.

- Do you have agreed goals?

- Are these goals measurable and achievable?

Setting safety goals

It is both obvious and easy to say that your goal is for the violent behaviour to stop, but how will you *know* it has stopped? What will be happening instead? Moving from a problem focus to a safety focus not only makes it clear what needs to happen but also helps develop a positive focus which takes into account the person's hopes and aspirations. Most people who have harmed others don't aspire to be violent. When you ask them how the violence has helped the situation, they often reply that it has not. A focus on constructive safety goals enables you to describe what outcomes are needed to reduce your concern, how you can measure them and how you can work together to achieve these goals.

PRACTICE ACTIVITY 4.3

Complete the chart below for 12-year-old Courtney who is currently with foster parents. List a constructive safe behaviour for each concern on the right side of the page. Use words such as 'do' rather than 'don't' and 'not'.

Concerns	Safety
Courtney kicks, hits and bites other children.	
She steals from the local shop.	
She swears at teachers.	
When upset, she trashes her bedroom.	

If you are Courtney's teacher, you may concentrate on in-school bullying. You could confront her with her behaviour – although she may well deny the offence – and set some sanctions, but how will you know when the bullying has ceased? How will you know that it hasn't simply moved to another setting? The solution focused approach to bullying is frequently either a whole-school or classroom approach where pupils and teachers are asked what their ideas are for a safe and happy environment; for example:

- What makes a safe playground?

- What does a safe playground look like?

- How is everyone behaving?

- How can you help someone remember what is okay and not okay in your safe playground?

- If someone is upsetting you, how can you tell them in a helpful way? Who else can you call on?

- What else needs to be happening so that more of this safer behaviour is happening in your playground?

- How can you keep yourself safe from allegations of bullying (for people who say, 'It wasn't me')?

When the pupils have agreed on a group goal of safety in the playground, you can write this up as a set of constructive rules (for an example of this, see Bateman and Milner 2015, p.148). Young (undated) suggests that a constructive goal will lead to more rapid progress than a negative one; for example, it is much more fruitful to organise a friendship group week than an anti-bullying one.

It is easier to measure whether or not goals have been achieved if you have defined them in clear, concrete behavioural changes, for example, 'I will talk to my teacher in a calm way; I will behave in a respectful way'. These broad goals are then developed by asking the person how they talk when they are calm: 'Suppose I looked through a window into your house and saw you being calm. What would I see, what would you be doing? What does being respectful look like?' This helps to ensure that there are no misunderstandings or misinterpretations by the worker of what calm and respectful behaviour means to the person. It also helps the person talk through what they will be actually doing when their best hopes are achieved, increasing their personal responsibility-taking. This breakdown will make the goals appear small and achievable in contrast to one large over-arching goal, which at the beginning of the work can feel unreachable and overwhelming.

It is important that all the people in the situation be consulted about their goals and that these are agreed. Husain was very frustrated at only being allowed to see his 6-year-old son, Kaleem, at supervised contact sessions at a local family centre where it was arranged that he would arrive 10 minutes earlier than his ex-partner, Rebecca, and wait out of sight until she had dropped off Kaleem. Similarly, he had to wait out of sight until she had left at the end of the contact session. He was also resentful at having to pay for these sessions. He wanted to move on to unsupervised contact at his parents' home and blamed Rebecca's mother for the lack of progress: 'She's always had it in for me. She'll do anything to stop me from seeing my lad'.

Rebecca's experience of Husain's violence was still vivid, but her mother talked not so much about the physical assaults but rather her distress at seeing her daughter being spat upon and trying to keep her safe when Husain was banging on the door. In understanding her position, it is important to acknowledge how threatening this was for her as well as Rebecca before attempting to establish a goal. Understandably, she was dubious that Husain had the capacity for sustained change, her initial goal being to keep him out their lives as much as possible. Asking her and Rebecca what needed to happen that would satisfy them that Husain has changed and that contact with Kaleem would be safe enabled them to set achievable and measurable goals. Quite simply, they wanted him to lead a 'normal life, doing the mundane things like going to work and being responsible'. When asked what a 'normal life' would be like, they listed:

- Husain will be holding down a proper job (for at least 6 months).

- He will be supporting Kaleem financially, sending him letters and cards.

- There will be evidence that he is drink and drug free.

- He will not be in trouble with the police.

- He will have a settled address.

- He will be handling frustration without losing his temper.

Rebecca prioritised 'handling frustration' as her most important goal as her experience of Husain was that 'he's fine when things are going right for him but is unable to keep this up when under pressure'. Husain was able to agree to these clear goals, which he considered were entirely reasonable.

PRACTICE ACTIVITY 4.4

The first five goals listed above are easy to measure, the sixth less so.

- How could you break this goal down into smaller, clear behavioural sections?

- How would you measure success in Husain meeting this goal?

- What would he be doing that would convince you that it would be safe for him to see Kaleem without supervision?

PRACTICE ACTIVITY 4.5

Jermaine had been moody and impatient for years. This had affected lots of people; he would hit people in pubs (he used to be a heavy drinker) and at work, if they annoyed him. He had been like this with Natalie too. Lots of the time, Natalie had felt like she was treading on eggshells. He had blackened her eyes and harmed her physically in other ways also, but when he kicked her down the stairs, dragged her into the sitting room, threw her on the floor and stamped on her, Natalie finally called the police. Jermaine pleaded guilty and served a 2-month prison sentence.

About half way through his prison sentence, Jermaine decided that he had hurt Natalie enough and that he would change. Since then, he hopes to be a better person, drinking less and handling his anger. Natalie would like him to be more approachable, listen more so that he can consider other people's feelings, help people he should be helping and spend more time with his family, instead of being in the pub.

- Are these goals achievable?

- Are they measurable?

- If so, how would you measure them?

Preferred futures

Turnell and Edwards (1999, p.71) state:

> The worker who broadens his/her focus beyond the maltreatment issue, and even beyond safety, and shows a genuine interest in the family's aspirations for their life, both immediate and longer term, stands a good chance of creating another territory in which a strong connection can be built. Most people, not surprisingly, are responsive to the worker who shows a genuine interest in what they want to achieve.

Asking people about their personal goals, their best hopes and aspirations, helps them begin to talk about a violence-free future. Questions include the following:

- What sort of person do you want to be?

- What can you see yourself doing when you will be doing [the goal], right here today?

- What will people notice that will be different when you are doing [the goal]?

- How might they respond differently to you?

- How do you think this will be helpful to you?

- When will be the first opportunity to do [the goal]?

- How will you know when you don't need to come here?

- How will I know that you don't need to come here any more?

It is important to go slowly and help the person elaborate on their answers to these questions, because they are not easy to answer. (You can test this by answering them yourself.) Often a person's initial answer will be quite vague. For example, Shane, who had been referred for violent temper outbursts at home, said he wanted to 'be working, being my normal self'. He was asked what 'being his normal self' would look like, but his goals remained vague: 'No worries on my mind. A normal 17-year-old who gets up and goes to work and sees his mates at the weekend'. Gradually, he began to talk about being free of his temper, but again his goal was still vague as it emerged that he's not the only person in his family who is violent, and he fears that, although he can look after himself, one day he'll come up against someone who is bigger and better. Gradually, it was possible to tease out a clearer aspiration:

> I would like to be someone who can look after himself and his family – basically, like my dad. He's had a hard life, but he's come out on top. But he's not in control of his temper when he's had a bit of beer.... . I do want to be like my dad, but I don't want his temper.

After talking about the ways he was like his dad, how he differed from him and which bits he wanted to keep and which to develop further (see the 'family differentiation' exercise, Dolan 1998, p.126), Shane worked out that his goal was to dispose of the family-temper heirloom. (For more details, see Milner and O'Byrne 2002, pp.67–69.)

Another way of helping people clarify their goal is to ask them more questions about the future, such as: 'Suppose I bump into you 2 years from now and see that you look really happy…what would you be doing that is different from today?' Alternatively, you could ask the person to imagine writing a letter from the future to someone who is important to them but with whom they may have lost touch. Then ask them where they are living, with whom, what they are doing, what the room looks like, whose photographs are on the wall and so forth, and then you will have their detailed, measurable goal. You could also take them in a time machine to their future home and ask them to look at themselves through the window. To obtain their solution in the letter-writing scenario, say that as they have been out of touch with this friend, the friend will be curious to learn how life became so good and will want to know how they did it. In the time-machine scenario ask, 'You know how it is when someone is watching you? They get a sense of it, so you turn round and see yourself peering through the window. She or he says to you "Oh, gosh, it's me when I was in all that trouble. Come in, come in". You say, "I haven't got long because I'm seeing this person about it all in a minute. But I must know, how *did* you do it?"'

PRACTICE EXAMPLE 4.1

Nineteen-year-old Carl, whom we met in Chapter 1 talking about the excitement of drop-kicking people with his ice skates, described a preferred future which was all about being a caring father:

Carl: I'd be sitting in a studio room with everything nice around me. Nice plain room just how I want it. I can see the baby with me but not Katie (his pregnant girlfriend). It's a room in a flat. I've always liked flats. I'm buying it. Two bedrooms. Downstairs flat. No garden. I hate gardening. The room's white with a bit of red to show my colours. Same throughout the flat, the floors the same...pine, or something pine coloured. Definitely pine furniture. Baby's room is full of things for it to play, but not so full that it'll get spoiled. A lot of educational things.

Judith: Whose photos are on the wall?

Carl: Picture of Katie in the room. I wouldn't stop Katie from seeing the baby.

Judith: Whose names are in your phone?

Carl: Names of parents, grandparents, best mate, work, baby's mum. And doctor...and hospital and things like that. I'm frightened of the baby being poorly already.

Judith: Any pets?

Carl: One dog...I'm fully trained for my job so I earn serious money and I'd have...Katie's been on about returning to work after the baby, so I could pay for a child minder in the morning and Katie would have him in the afternoon. Sometimes to stay overnight.

Judith: So, tell me, how did you do all this?

Carl: Sit down and talk it out. Throw myself into work and learn as much as I can, and prepare for the baby. Also get out of the environment I'm in at the moment. Stay with mum, get on better with my stepdad. No more drinking...no fights.

Judith: What will you do instead when you see red?

Carl: Breathe deeply and think about the baby. Thinking about the baby helps. Main thing that comes to mind is the picture of the scan. I care for the baby, big time, if no one else. Think baby, baby, baby.

Focusing on developing Carl's goal of being a caring, responsible father enabled him over the next 3 weeks to (a) begin listening to people, (b) show consideration, gain 95% control over his temper, (c) get a job with learning opportunities at his stepdad's workplace, (d) negotiate his way out of his current flat share, (e) improve his relationship with his mum, (f) talk things over with Katie so that he could still be a responsible father to their expected child even though their relationship was over, (g) cut down his drinking to two pints on weekend nights, (h) join a rugby club (where the coach complimented him on not retaliating to a deliberate elbow in his face) and (i) resist a wind up socially, leading his best mate to refer to him as a person who used to have a temper. Carl said, 'I feel good about myself. I got into a lot of conversations with people'. As time had been taken to clarify Carl's goals and solutions, breaking them down into small, concrete steps, it was possible for him to provide evidence of change which, in turn, inspired him to take more steps.

(Adapted from Milner 2001, pp.106–107)

Most people can answer this question 'How did you do it?' immediately because they have now been talking about their older, competent self at some length. For those who struggle to answer the question, they can be invited to ask their older, wiser self for advice on comfort: 'Okay, so you can't tell me *yet*, but can you tell me how you got through this difficult time?' This invites them to work out what would be comforting during the current difficulties. Additionally, because you added the word *yet* in this question, you are presupposing that the person will be able to answer the question in the future. Although we don't use a 'miracle question' much, preferring to talk about best hopes and preferred futures, many solution focused workers use it to elicit goals.

The miracle question

de Shazer (1988, p.5) gave the name 'miracle question' to any specific question that has been shown to work particularly well in developing goals. It is quite long and similar to a guided night-time fantasy, so it is especially useful in helping people who struggle to say what their best hopes are. We don't use the word 'miracle' when asking this question because when we work with children who may have been sexually abused, we are aware that associating words like 'miracle' or 'magic' with bedtime could be totally inappropriate in these instances. We use the words 'something wonderful' instead. Although it sounds formulaic, the miracle question works well because it is a curious question; you can never be sure what the answer will be. It goes like this:

> Now, I want to ask you a strange question. Suppose that while you are sleeping tonight and the entire house is quiet, a miracle happened. The miracle is that the problem which brought you here is solved. However, because you are sleeping, you don't know that the miracle has happened. So when you wake up tomorrow morning, what will be different that will tell you that the miracle has happened and the problem which brought you here has been solved?

This is a big question in that it is the start of a new story of how life is going to be for the person, so it helps to ask it in the following way:

- Speak slowly and gently to give the person time to shift from a problem focus to a solution focus.

- Mark the beginning of a solution-building process clearly by introducing the miracle question as unusual or strange.

- Use frequent pauses, allowing the person time to absorb the question and process his or her experiences through its different parts.

- Because the question asks for a description of the future, use future-directed words: What would be different? What will be signs of the miracle?

- When probing and asking follow-up questions, frequently repeat the phrase 'a miracle happens and the problem that brought you here is solved', in order to reinforce the transition to solution talk.

- When people lapse into problem talk, gently refocus their attention on what will be different in their lives when the miracle happens.

(Adapted from de Jong and Berg 2002, p.85)

In working with people who have harmed others, goal-setting questions must include the safety goals of the other people in their life. A question can be asked such as, 'What would you be doing that would make your children/partner feel safer?' or 'What would your mum/teacher notice different about you?' An answer may be very simple but still constitute a desirable and measurable goal, for example, 'I will be sitting at my desk listening to my teacher' or 'I will be eating my dinner at the table' or 'I will be listening to her'. Sometimes answers to the miracle question provide dramatic and immediate solutions, like when 10-year-old Ian said he would be coming downstairs with a smile on his face and his brother would not be teasing him at breakfast. His mother immediately commented that if he came downstairs with a smile on his face, she would stop his brother from teasing him. Despite Ian having long-standing, serious behaviour problems, he and his mother worked out both their goal and solution (better behaviour) from this one small conversation (Milner 2001, p.14). Equally, people often struggle to think what would be different, so we list below some follow-up questions.

Miracle question prompts

Miracle question prompts are as follows:

- What will you notice, what else, what else, what else?

- What will you see?

- What will be different?

- What will other people notice about you?

- Picture later in the morning, what is happening now, what else is telling you the miracle has happened?

- At school/home/work/the pub, what is different here?

- Back at home, late afternoon, what do you notice now?

- What sort of things are you saying to yourself at the end of the day?

For unrealistic answers like 'winning the lottery', 'all the teachers will have been sacked', 'he won't be winding me up', 'we'll have better managers', acknowledge that this has happened and then ask:

- So, what will *you* be doing differently then?

- Can any of this happen now?

Not all unrealistic answers are unrealistic: 'being off medication' or 'not having social workers in my life' are entirely reasonable goals, leading logically to the next question: 'So, what will you be doing differently when your doctor agrees for you to come off medication?' or 'What will you be doing differently when the social workers feel your child is safe?' Even where a person is psychotic, Hawkes, Marsh and Wilgosh (1998) maintain that bizarre or unrealistic responses to the miracle question are an acceptable starting place in solution finding. Using the example of someone hearing voices who has a goal of becoming England's next football manager, they detail the steps he would need to take to achieve that goal, all of which will involve taking responsibility.

PRACTICE ACTIVITY 4.6

Choose an aspect of work that causes you anxiety, for example, report writing, completing agency forms on time, planning lessons and so forth. Imagine that tonight you go home, have dinner and relax, then go to bed as usual where you fall into a deep, dreamless sleep. During the night, something wonderful happens, and the problems you have at work have disappeared completely. Because you are asleep, you do not know that this is the case.

- When you go to work in the morning, what will be the first thing you notice that will tell you that this wonderful thing has happened?

- What will your colleagues notice that is different?

- What will your supervisor notice that is different?

- What will you being doing differently?

(Adapted from Myers 2007, p.59)

PRACTICE EXAMPLE 4.2

Lynne has had a lot of loss in her life recently. First she lost her baby and her job, then her partner, Robert, lost his job after damaging his back. They have both started drinking more than they think is good for them. At the moment her confidence is very low. This makes her aggressive with Robert and people who run her down (mostly her family). Smacking people makes Lynne feel better for about 5 minutes, but she feels bad afterwards.

Lynne says that her miracle day is one where:

I wake up wanting to get out of bed. I'd have a smile on my face while I'm making breakfast and I'm looking forward to doing the cleaning and washing up. I'd be in a good mood, vacuuming and polishing to music. I'd leave Robert to get up when he wants. Then I'd put on a smart green top and tie my hair back and go out to Morrison's, or to see my mum and dad or get some DIY stuff. ('What if you meet any of your family who put you down?') I'd ask them how they are doing and be nice to them. ('What will you be doing later?') I'd be decorating my bedroom...in traditional chintzy blues and greens. The kids help when they come home from school because they like it when their mum is buzzing, all excited. Afterwards, we'll all have a shepherd's pie made with condensed tomato soup with cheese on top, wash up, watch some television and think what a good day it has been. No drinking...I'd have been too busy buzzing to bother with drinking.

There are several variants of the miracle question, but shortened or crystal ball versions do not seem to work as well, probably because they don't encourage enough detail of what will be different. This detail is important in helping people discover solutions and ideas they did not know they had and helps them talk themselves into change. Goals also expand as progress is made and hope increases. This is fine as long as these goals are achievable and measurable.

Group miracle questions

The miracle question can also be used with groups of young people. Sharry (2001, p.136) suggests asking group members to close their eyes, relax each muscle in turn and visualise a relaxing scene before asking the miracle question. Then they are asked to imagine the new solution situation in detail:

> You are going to be surprised at all the differences and changes you notice... So what do you notice first?... What tells you the miracle has happened?... How do you feel different?... What do you notice is different about other people?...

After the visualisation process, members discuss the differences in pairs, and then in the whole group. The advantage of this is that the solutions generated by group members are likely to have common links, and this can be reinforcing when shared in the whole group. Also, hearing other people's miracles can be motivating, inspiring and encourage people to develop their own. Don't worry if the group format encourages silliness; it will start the group thinking, and they may need time to work out their goals. With people who are mandated by the court to attend a group, Lee and colleagues (2003) give the group the task of formulating a goal that will be useful to them, cause others to notice a change in them, and involve a new and different behaviour. They find that some people grasp the idea quickly while others find it more difficult to develop goals, so it is important to be patient and wait for responses: 'filling any uncomfortable silences only displays a lack of confidence in the participants' abilities to begin the process' (p.58). Inevitably, if you wait, the vacuum will be filled by a participant's ideas.

Shortened circular miracle question

The shortened circular miracle question is particularly useful with families when you suspect that some family members are afraid and/ or reluctant to voice their opinions, or where you are unsure whether the children's opinions are their own or unduly influenced by their parents' views.

Before we ask the miracle question, we give everyone a piece of paper and a pencil and ask them to write down the answer to the question we are about to ask. Preschool children are invited to draw their answer; very young children are given a sheet of paper, stickers and crayons to make a picture which they can then present to an adult; and any older children without speech are linked with another family member whom the family has identified as the person best able to represent them. We keep this light-hearted by reminding them that no one must see their answer and to put their arm round the paper as they would do at school to prevent copying. Then we ask:

> Suppose, while you are asleep tonight, a wonderful thing happens and everything that is worrying you [or your teachers, or Social Care and so forth] has disappeared. But because you were fast asleep, you didn't notice this happening. Write down the first thing that you would notice that would tell you that things are better?

Reminding everyone to keep their answers hidden, we then ask them in turn to guess what another person has written. This is not done randomly; we ask the most supportive parent to guess what the youngest child has said as this is relatively non-threatening and gives that parent the opportunity to demonstrate his or her understanding of the child's needs and wishes. Then we ask the most confident child to guess what the most powerful family member may have put. Finally, we ask this family member what they think another child has said. (We usually select the most vulnerable child here.) Where families give superficial answers, such as 'He would have a new bike', we consult the family pet, and even if it has to be an imaginary one, the family will know what its goals will be. After this has been talked about, we ask each person what they actually put and discuss differences of perceptions. This exercise has several advantages:

- It gives children the opportunity to express their needs and wishes.

- It enables parents to hear these needs and wishes.

- It encourages discussion about what changes can be made.

- It enables a parent to discuss differences of opinion without fear of being contradicted or put down.

- It provides a snapshot of family dynamics in action.

The latter observations are important as they reveal family strengths (for example, a parent being unexpectedly caring toward a child) and areas for improvement (for example, the children fighting and the parents unable to handle this). It is less threatening to explore an area for improvement as a possible goal during the exercise, and parents enjoy their competencies being noticed and commented upon. Numerous hopes usually emerge, so it is important to highlight what would be the first sign of the goals happening, and prioritise all the goals. This will ensure that no one becomes overwhelmed or confused with that toward which they are working. This exercise is complicated as you are moving from what someone thinks another has written to what they have *actually* written, and it is likely that there will be a lot of comment about people's replies, so be prepared to write down the answers. It helps if you have a list of people's names and room for the initial guess answers and the actual answer. These notes will form the basis of your goal exploration, for example, 'What will you be doing differently when your goals all match?'

Where the problem is denied

A child once asked us what probation was, and on being told that instead of being sent to prison the person was given the chance to talk to a worker for a few weeks about the things they have done wrong, the child replied, feelingly, 'I'd rather go to prison'. None of us like having our shortcomings picked over again and again, so it is not surprising that people who have harmed others are often defensive in an effort to avoid humiliation. This does not mean that you can't work with them; it simply means that you need to offer invitations. We have talked earlier about showing an interest in their wider hopes and aspirations and bypass the defensiveness by questions such as:

- What is more important to you, to be believed or get out of this mess?

- These things have been said about you and mud sticks, so what can you do differently that will keep you safe from allegations like these in the future?

- These are the concerns (list them) that worry other people, so what will you be doing when they are no longer worried?

- You say you are safe around your children, so what hard evidence of your safe behaviour is there to convince the judge?

When working with denied child abuse, Turnell and Essex (2006) provide a framework for talking with parents and children. They keep out of the denial dispute by suggesting it is left on an imaginary shelf:

> My place in all this is to take the concerns social services have seriously and help you to show them that nothing like that can happen in the future so that you have a chance to get your family back together. So is it okay if we leave those issues on that shelf? (p.56)

Doing this does not get in the way of talking about the concerns – who's worried, what are they worried about, what happened then and what are we doing – which remain central to the work.

Other useful questions are as follows:

- That's great, we both see the need to make your child safe. You know your child and your family better than we do. What ideas do you have for making your child safer?

- What do you think it would take to make your children safer?

- For our involvement with your family to be useful to you, what would need to happen? What would change in your family? What would change about your partner/your child?

- How have you solved these sorts of problems before? How were you able to do that? Could you do it again?

- It's really clear to us that you don't want us continually in your life. What do you think we need to see to close the case and get out of your life?

(Adapted from Turnell and Edwards 1999, pp.68–69)

Where there are conflicting goals

Where violence is committed on a stranger, the goal setting is straightforward: to either help the person become safe in the future or remove them from the community. We have found that victims of stranger attacks usually recover more quickly than when the violence takes place in a relationship – regardless of the severity of the physical violence. Indeed, we haven't found that the severity of the violence is relevant to outcomes, many people telling us that the verbal and emotional violence hurts more: 'A split lip is a split lip. You get over that. But the look of hatred on his face…that really scared me'. So it's not surprising that people have different goals, like Natalie earlier: she wanted not to get hit, but she also wanted Jermaine to be more approachable. In our work with domestic violence we have found the 'overcoming violence' chart helpful for widening out goals, with being listened to important for both men and women: 'He asks me what is wrong and I say nothing. I just want some space but he goes on and on and then he gets angry and hits me'. 'When I can't get my point of view over, my words get all muddled and I get confused. Then I get shaky…it's like a tight feeling in my chest and then I get angry…shouting first, then pushing, punching…mostly walls but sometimes Linda…throwing things and then walking out'. Mostly people don't want the violent person removed from their lives, they want that person to be respectful to them.

It is almost impossible to agree on goals where there is no respect – where one person is contemptuous of the other. Often we hear people referring to the other person as 'the bitch', 'she', 'that bastard' and so forth – objectifying them: 'Once the other was seen as a subject, maybe even with compassion, but they have now become an obstacle. Everything would be better if the other was no longer there. The other person, in this way, is always seen as less' (Bannink 2010, p.55). This lack of respect is usually most acute in bitter post-divorce conflicts, with friends and relatives taking sides and magnifying the 'problem behaviours' of the other partner. The increasingly bitter residential parent begins to use the children as weapons to harm the ex-partner. When we have observed children's contact with the non-residential parent, they often change from playing happily to becoming cool and withdrawn as the session draws to a close. This enables them to return to the residential parents without showing any signs of having enjoyed themselves; something they have learned will annoy or upset that parent. Where children are unable to develop psychological separateness, they side psychologically with the residential parent. Usually the eldest child begins this process, gradually drawing in the younger ones.

PRACTICE EXAMPLE 4.3

Mina (9 years old) and Rajinder (6 years old) lived with their mother, Asha, after Asha and Dev's marriage broke down, as she kept the family home and Dev lived temporarily with a cousin. Initially there were few problems with the children seeing their father alternate Saturdays for a few hours in town. After Dev obtained employment, a house and a new partner with two girls – Sara (10 years old) and Laila (8 years old) – Asha, who also had a new partner, refused to let the girls see their father at his new home on the grounds that Dev had always been violent and that the girls were only safe if contact was in public, and that they didn't know Sara and Laila. She reluctantly agreed to an initial contact with Sara, Laila and their mother, Surinderjit, at the local Sikh temple with a view to Dev joining them there at a later contact if all went well.

All four girls were nicely dressed with beautiful scarves on their heads. Sara and Laila brought gifts which Mina and Rajinder opened. They said thank you for the gifts, but Rajinder was more enthusiastic and quickly joined in play with Sara and Laila. Mina sat quietly, speaking when Surinderjit spoke to her, but not volunteering anything.

Two weeks later, Mina and Rajinder arrived at the next contact scruffily dressed, in sharp contrast to Sara and Laila. Mina sat with her head down, speaking to no one. Rajinder began to play with Laila, but after seeing that her sister would not join in, she too sat with her head down.

PRACTICE ACTIVITY 4.7

Think back to a period in your life when you had a problem or a conflict.

- How did you resolve these difficulties then?

- Think of at least three things that you did that were helpful.

- If you currently have a conflict, which of those former ways could you use again in your current situation?

(Adapted from Bannink 2010, p.32)

Useful questions to ask before attempting any goal setting in a situation such as the case example above would be to ask Asha:

- Does this way of being suit you?

- What effect do you think it is having on the children?

- What do the children understand is happening between you right now?

- How determined are you to take action to reduce the conflict?

- What hopes have you for reducing the conflict?

- When it is dumped, how will you be talking about the children?

- How long will it take to get goodwill back?

- What other ideas can you think of for resolving this situation?

- How would you have dealt with this sort of problem in the past when things were better for you?

(Adapted from Bannink 2010; Watling 2012)

Where the conflict has escalated to the extent that the goal of one parent is not to enforce their own interests but to destroy or damage the other by alienating the children from the other parent, it is all too easy for the worker to vilify that parent. But this is to objectify them, to be as contemptuous toward them as they are to their ex-partner and see them as the enemy – especially when the worker is moved by the effects on the children. The alienating parent's position needs to be understood and acknowledged too. Relationship breakdowns are grounded in resentments of emotional bullying, physical hurts, infidelity, financial inequalities and so forth. Separating a household usually involves some financial hardship, and the partner who moves out may lose touch with the children for a short time while they sort out their living arrangements. Their reappearance on the scene asking for contact is often met with resentment.

In these instances, resentment can be externalised as an enemy with questions such as:

- How would you name the feelings of resentment/unfairness that bother you?

- Can you tell me about times when (selected resentment) is not there, or less?

- When it is present, how do you deal with it?

During our conversation about resentment, a man said to us, 'I get it; it's like putting another bean in the resentment jar'. We talked about how maybe he didn't want to let go of all his resentments, but perhaps he would have a rule that he couldn't put a new bean in the resentment jar until he'd taken one out. This stops resentments from escalating and takes some of the strong feelings out of the situation; it's hard to be furious about something when you're working with a jar of beans (however imaginary).

Another way of reducing resentments is to get all the parties together in a neutral place. We tend to choose an open-sided cafe in a shopping mall as this provides a setting where people can't start raising their voices but they *can* walk off for a while without it looking like a tantrum. We begin by asking each person to say one thing they resent most, and why, and for the other person to listen to this and reply sympathetically. We then ask them to park the resentment so we can proceed with their best hopes. We have followed up such meetings with group-contact sessions, such as everyone – parents, children, new partners and their children, grandparents – all going bowling or swimming. To prevent the group from splitting down resentment lines, we team participants up differently; for example, girls versus boys in bowling, one parent looks after all the little ones in swimming while the other takes on the deep end with the more confident swimmers. Unlike contact sessions where the children leave one home to visit another, these group sessions remove the anxiety of 'reporting back' when children return to the main home, as both parents know exactly what happened as they were there. This way trust can develop.

Where there is no progress and the alienating parent raises the bar by objectifying the other parent as a child abuser, there is no safety for the children from emotional harm and the matter needs swift referral to the court. The court's powers are actually limited, as to imprison a parent for non-compliance with a Contact Order would simply alienate the children further, and making a Residence Order in favour of the alienated parent increases the resentments. However, a threat to treat this as a child protection issue, with the possibility of the children being accommodated so that both parents could have supervised contact to enable workers to see how they reacted with each other and their parents, is remarkably effective. In the case of Asha (see Practice example 4.3) the children became increasingly alienated, but a recommendation for care proceedings in the draft court report brought a rapid change of heart. Mina and Rajinder were enjoying regular contact with their father within 2 weeks of Asha reading the report – which obviously was then amended for the hearing.

People with learning difficulties

When we are starting work with people with learning difficulties, we are often told that they don't concentrate well. We find that people with learning difficulties can concentrate for 30–40 minutes as long as we remember to go at a suitable pace, use appropriate materials and make it fun. People with learning difficulties do not function well at all when they are stressed, so we allow 10 minutes of settling-down time. The basic principle is to reduce the speed of everything by:

- talking more slowly and repeating or rephrasing important points several times

- using pictures or symbols to explain complex concepts such as thoughts and emotions

- explaining ourselves through written or drawn materials as this method of communicating is less threatening than face-to-face conversations. (For more details, see Bateman and Milner 2015.)

It takes time to learn new behaviours, so short chunks of information need to be repeated several times and in fresh ways. Charts and stickers act as useful visual reminders. To help the person understand new situations, we keep changes to the minimum. We also provide opportunities to practise newly learned behaviours.

Chapter 5

Discovering Strengths and Resources

Turning deficits into resources

Alcoholics Anonymous (1976, p.451) states:

> 'When I focus on what's good today, I have a good day, and when I focus on what is bad, I have a bad day. If I focus on a problem, the problem increases; if I focus on the answer, the answer increases'.

A constant focus on what has gone wrong is discouraging and distressing for people, especially people who have been violent. Assessing their dangerousness looms so large that rarely are they told what they are doing well and come to believe that there is nothing good about them. Psychopathological reports add to this process; for example, a man we worked with was devastated when he read the results of his psychological assessment, which concluded as follows: 'Given his personality difficulties and the long-standing nature of his interpersonal problems, change is likely to be difficult to achieve...the prognosis is poor'. Such comments do not aid the therapeutic process as recipients tend to resist hearing bad things about themselves, or become depressed. Where there is a parenting assessment focusing on the history of what has gone wrong in people's lives, this negativity also affects the people who have been on the receiving end of violence.

PRACTICE EXAMPLE 5.1

Helen found being asked for details of Danny's assaults on her triggered flashbacks and panic attacks. Insensitive questions about her previous failed relationships – hinting that perhaps she was drawn to people who are violent – and the early stages of their relationship triggered her insecurity, fuelling the jealous thoughts she was struggling to control. Danny resisted talking about his childhood to social workers as he held previous social workers responsible for his very unhappy experiences in care. Helen's reluctance to talk openly with the assessing social workers was seen by them as denial and collusion with Danny to hide the reality of domestic violence so that they could get their child back from care, leading to further challenging and more reluctance on Helen's part. Danny's sullen resistance to questions about his childhood was seen as further evidence of his dangerousness, with the social workers making comments that he was using his body language in an attempt to intimidate them.

(For more details, see Milner 2008.)

Meetings and case conferences increase negative viewpoints as each participant adds a comment that builds the problem. The worker ends up with a very bleak picture, what White (1995) refers to as a *problem saturated description*, which leads to workers feeling helpless in the face of the enormity of the problem situation. Turnell and Edwards (1999) recommend that workers expand the picture, exploring people's strengths and resources. This is not to minimise the violence; rather, it validates the totality of people's experiences, places current problems in context – few people are completely evil – and makes contact with workers less threatening. More importantly, it helps the violent person develop a more competent, caring self; in other words, it's much easier to do more of something that's working than stop doing what is considered problematic. For example, the man whose prognosis was considered *poor* was asked to consult his family about things they liked about him, away from the violence. His son surprised him by saying he liked his dad's resilience (his own words), his explanations and playing football with him. This not only reminded the man of competent fathering skills that could be further developed but – importantly – it gave his son permission to talk about his father's behaviour. The boy was soon confident enough to tell his dad what made him feel unsafe too.

Solution focused approaches presume that everyone, including not just the individuals who have been violent but also those who may have been subjected to it, has strengths, resources and abilities that can be used to develop a violence-free future. The solution focused practitioner will be keen to explore those attributes, skills and behaviours that the person has that can be marshalled to challenge the violence and increase safety, recognising that the resources people have can be effective in promoting and sustaining change. This is a skilled activity that requires concentration and discipline, ensuring that we are asking the right questions in the right way and able to hear the answers, excavating hidden strengths that are often obscured or neglected. Wheeler (2005) nicely describes this process as *panning for gold*, that is, helping to recognise the tiniest glimmer of hope in what can otherwise be a story of misery, defeat and deficit.

This strengths perspective moves us away from focusing on the deficits that will be all too apparent in lives where violence is present, be they poor childhood, emotional blockages, hypermasculinity or the many other explanations that are commonplace, all of which highlight problems and reinforce negativity. The search for strengths is not simply a 'feel-good' exercise; they are sought so that they can be considered as part of the strategy to deal with the violence. They are 'examined as competencies that the person can utilize in the search for a satisfactory and enduring solution' (Myers and Milner 2007, pp.136–137), although improving someone's self-esteem does assist them to take a more measured look at the world.

PRACTICE ACTIVITY 5.1

The next time you are due to have the first meeting with someone to discuss their violent behaviour, try to think of the strengths you already know they have.

- What does the referral information tell you about their positive abilities?

- What qualities do they have?

- What might you want to ask them to find out more about these qualities?

If we accept that people have strengths, resources and abilities to deal with violence, then we need to look for them, that is, become the 'solution detectives' of Sharry, Madden and Darmody (2012). Our experience tells us that quite often people are thoroughly demoralised by the time they come to us: having been told that they are unpleasant, aggressive, 'bad' people, they have internalised this and behave to expectations or passively accept their fate. There are dominant stories about violence that make people 'monsters' or locate the problem within them, which makes it hard to see how change can happen. In Chapter 3 we looked at how this can be undermined and how the story of totalising violence is just that, a story, and one that can be rewritten when we find *exceptions* to this behaviour. Searching for strengths is the partner of searching for exceptions, and quite often the two processes overlap. The major difference is that it is possible to look outside the violence/absence-of-violence conversations to explore other sources of skills that can be brought in to resist the behaviour. Seemingly unrelated activities might well provide ideas for how they can be translated into building a problem-free future. So how do we go about this? We are great believers in asking people helpful questions, and also in *really* looking for those strengths that are hidden.

Starting a strengths conversation

Holding a productive conversation about a person's strengths and resources is made easier by making a deliberate shift from problem talk. You could say something like, 'You've told me a lot about what is getting you into trouble, but if we are going to fix it, I need to know what's going well for you right now. Then we can use what's going well to fix all this stuff that's not going so well'. Alternatively, you can simply ask the person to tell you what the good things about them are. We all find this difficult to do as supervision usually focuses on what is going wrong. Sadly, people who are violent often tell us there isn't *anything* good about them, so we ask questions such as:

- What would your friends say are the good things about you?

- What would your mum/dad/grandma say are the good things about you? (We like to consult grandmas as often people have a supportive 'nan'.)

- What would your favourite teacher say?

- If your pet could talk, what would it say are the good things about you?

- In what are you interested?

- What do you enjoy doing?

- At what are you good?

Alternatively, we hand the person a sheet of paper with 1–20 marked on the left side of the paper and ask them to come back when they have consulted people and pets in their life and found out 20 good things about themselves. The inclusion of others in identifying, recognising and authenticating strengths and resources contributes greatly to how people perceive themselves and gives them hope for a more satisfying future.

You then follow up any answer with an expression of curiosity about how the person did that, identifying the skills, personal qualities and resources they used, however small or insignificant. For example, a man who told us there was nothing good about him came for a second appointment with a full list of 20 items. He announced triumphantly that he hadn't expected to be able to find out any good thing, but on looking at it, he noticed that we had accidentally omitted item 19. So he promptly wrote down that he was observant, which got him off to a flying start. A strengths conversation is not limited to the so-called social skills; any ability, skill or achievement is relevant. A person's skill in growing prize dahlias, for example, tells you that the person has patience, attention to detail, reliability and research skills – and that's just for starters. It is important to take your time over a strengths conversation as people find it very strange at first. Furthermore, people who can't take criticism are often the worst at taking praise and pride in their achievements. It is your task to dig out strengths and resources to be used in solution finding, and much persistence is needed.

PRACTICE EXAMPLE 5.2

Jared, aged 14 years, had sexually abused his younger sibling and was given a community order to see a sex offender specialist. He was an overweight boy who was academically not very good at school, poor at physical sports, unpopular with his peers, despaired of by his teachers, rejected by his father and the focus of anger from his mother and other family members. His social worker thought that he was surly, uncooperative, thoroughly unpleasant, racist and had a high risk of reoffending.

He came to the first meeting and this was acknowledged for doing so, as he had made his own way across the city to the office to discuss his sexual misbehaviour with his worker. He was asked what he was good at, but he could not identify anything about himself about which he was remotely positive. Jared was set a homework task to complete before his next session the following week: he had to make a list of the 20 things he was good at, even just a little bit. He could accept that one quality was that he had taken his visit to the office seriously, so he had some responsibility-taking attributes. He was asked to canvass the opinions of others about his good qualities, and although anxious, he agreed to talk to his mother and siblings to see if there were any positive things, however small. He felt that this list would still be shorter than necessary, so he explored from where he might get further information. Knowing that the family had a dog, the worker asked what it would say about him if it could talk. Jared said that the dog would say that he loved it. As 'love' is an imprecise concept, Jared was asked how the dog knew that he loved it, and he said that he made a fuss of it every time he came home from school. The worker suggested that Jared interview the dog for any other attributes he might have, and perhaps he could interview the family goldfish as well.

At the next session Jared came with a list of his 20 qualities. These qualities included being able to recognise when the dog needed to be let out, taking the dog for a walk and keeping him on the leash and scooping out the large amounts of fish food that his younger sister had enthusiastically put in the goldfish bowl – all of which had come from 'interviews' with the dog and the goldfish. It was agreed that Jared had been developing strengths of (a) being observant of, and acting on, the needs of others, and (b) taking appropriate responsibility and putting things right. These strengths were the basis for a discussion about how he could build on them to continue a problem-free future.

PRACTICE ACTIVITY 5.2

- Make a list of all your best skills (don't be modest).
- How do these help you to be helpful with the people with whom you work?
- Choose one of these skills.
- How can you enhance this skill to make it a bit more effective?
- What would you have to do?

- When can you do it by?

- How would your work colleagues know that you are doing it better?

(Myers 2007, p.9)

It is rarely sufficient to help the violent person identify strengths and resources that can be used to find solutions; the people who have been on the receiving end of the violence may need assistance in recognising these strengths and resources. Colin, a year nine pupil at a grammar school, had a history of fighting, being disruptive in class, abusing teachers and failing to do any work. The final straw for his teachers was when he was caught shoplifting in school uniform and he received a fixed-term exclusion. His head teacher reported that he was very pessimistic about Colin's future as he was associating with a bad crowd outside school, had a difficult family background, was a persistent liar and showed no remorse for his wrongdoings. School didn't want to readmit Colin until he admitted his wrongdoings and showed remorse (case example adapted from Durrant 1993, pp.66–67). It is not unreasonable to assume that Colin will respond to his school's demands with a defiant, 'don't care' attitude, and should you discover the strengths and resources which Colin has and develop them to change his behaviour, he has been storied in a such a negative way that teachers are not likely to have any faith in his reform. They are more likely to be on the lookout for behaviours which confirm their original assessment. It can be helpful to ask his teachers for exceptions to his problem behaviour and what good things they have noticed about him, but this will take patience, persistence and *tact*. They have had a great deal to put up with from Colin and this needs to be acknowledged. In these sorts of situations, we tweak existing disciplinary methods. For example, where a school uses a lesson-by-lesson report card, we adapt it so that it has two identical sides. At the bottom of one side it reads 'Please make a note of everything Colin has done right in your lesson'. On the other, identical side, it reads 'Please make a note of everything Colin has done wrong in your lesson, but not until you have made a comment on the other side'. This not only helps the teacher notice Colin's good points and efforts, but it also motivates Colin to force the teacher into making a positive comment, and to do this he has to behave well.

PRACTICE EXAMPLE 5.3

Judith attended a school meeting about a boy who was close to being excluded because of his aggressive behaviour. The boy did not turn up for the meeting. The teachers were extremely negative about the boy and could not see any redeeming features, only the problems that he was causing them and the other students. When asked, they said that they could not see any strengths and quickly reverted to highlighting the problem behaviours.

Judith decided to take a calculated chance and asked the following question: 'God forbid, but if the boy was run over and killed this afternoon, and you were asked to deliver a eulogy at his funeral next week, what would you say about him?'

The teachers thought about this and then began to find some times when he had been less of a problem and some of his (small, but still there) strengths, skills and attributes.

Strengths in adversity

Strengths can be found even in adversity, and complimenting people is often a good way to start any solution focused session as there is always some positive element to highlight, and it also keeps the worker focused on solutions. In the case of Jared (see Practice example 5.2), he had made his way across the city in the full knowledge that he would have to talk about intimate and embarrassing personal issues to a complete stranger, that the worker would probably dislike him as much as his social worker did and that if he didn't go, he might get sent to jail or taken into care. (Children often do not differentiate between the two.) The very fact that he arrived and was prepared to give it a go said something about his commitment and provided the beginnings of appropriate responsibility-taking. (We say 'appropriate' because it is unfair to expect a child to take the same level of responsibility for their behaviour as an adult; see Bateman and Milner 2015.) When he arrived at the office, his worker was able to say that she had noticed that Jared had got there on time and wondered how he had managed to do this, affirming his achievement and expanding the possibility for a strengths talk.

Even when people have experienced significant adverse life events, they can be encouraged to explore obscured strengths and resources. Coping or survival questions can be used to begin to elicit those times when people have struggled against the problem and are 'a form of solution talk that has been tailored to make sense to clients who are feeling overwhelmed' (de Jong and Berg 2002, p.224). For example, someone who has been the subject of sustained domestic violence and cannot see any way forward might be asked, 'What does it say about you that you are able to be here today and tell me this?' or 'Despite all this you have managed to keep your family together and ask for help; how did you do this?' – which are questions that contain hope and recognise that people are resilient. The notion of 'coping' here is not about 'putting up' with an intolerable situation, but rather how people have managed to bring their personal skills and resources to deal with the problem, even on a temporary or limited basis. It is these strengths that are then explored to see how they can be used to develop solutions.

PRACTICE EXAMPLE 5.4

Sahida was at her wits' end with the behaviour of her teenage son, Arun, as he was physically attacking her and her other children. She said that this had been happening for some time and had now worn her down to the point where she felt that she was a bad parent and all her children should be taken into care. The worker asked Sahida how she had managed to ensure that the children were looked after so well, as they were well fed and well clothed, were doing okay at school and their health was fine. Sahida began to describe the strength she gained from her religion and how this had helped her to keep on trying to 'do the right thing'. She agreed that she was a determined person who had persevered for a long time and was able to see that her parenting had been positive. These were strengths that formed the basis for further discussions about what else might work and what had already made a small difference.

People who are depressed by their circumstances can be invited to think about how they are coping, so questions may look like this:

- Given all that has happened to you and how you feel at the moment, how did you manage to get out of bed this morning?

- What does it say about you that you managed to get out of bed, dress and come all this way to talk with me?

- How have you managed to cope for so long?

- What has prevented it from being worse?

- You say that you feel like killing yourself. What has helped you to stay alive?

Complicating stories

People can be storied as problematic by their loved ones, which makes marshalling their support more difficult. For example, with the families of children who have sexual behaviour problems, we would comment on all the positive behaviours their child showed in the session, such as the child's ability to listen, be polite, answer questions, show an interest and so forth. Then we would say to the parents, 'You must be doing something very right'. This is surprising to them as they may well have storied their child as a problem to avoid being seen as failing parents, and they will probably say something like, 'You should see him at home' – at which point you can just smile and move on to another topic. You have sown the seed for strengths' noticing, both parental and child strengths. It can be even harder to convince some *workers* of a person's strengths. Turnell and Edwards (1999) comment that some strengths are sometimes viewed as negatives in that the worker suspects the person is putting on an act. Clark (2013) notes that some workers worry about false compliance. He adds: 'Compliance… cannot rest as a final goal. Behavior change is always in ascendancy with strengths based practice' (p.143). So it is important when talking about a person's strengths to talk about how those strengths relate to safety. The search for strengths and resources is not simply to list them on one side of the page; it is to use them to develop different ways of being and evidence this.

Group strengths and resources

Strengths are not necessarily individual: when approached in a solution focused way, 'anti-bullying is a dynamic and rewarding area of positive activity that validates whatever the existing skills are in a school and uses them as resources to reach its greatest potential' (Young undated, p.26). Young goes on to say that in schools with few strengths, it is vitally important to identify them so that they can be capitalised upon. The same is true of any organisation with bullying issues. Questions that elicit group skills include:

- What is going well in our organisation?

- What do we do that helps people feel safe?

- What *don't* we want to change about our organisation?

- What are we most proud of in this organisation?

- How do we give credit to people?

- How do we look after our workforce?

- What would our customers say is the best thing about us?

- What are our support networks?

PRACTICE ACTIVITY 5.3 (EVER APPRECIATING CIRCLES)

Purpose:

- To allow you to notice the minutiae of competencies in your daily situations.

- To help you learn to look at the world with an appreciative eye rather than focusing on deficits.

Look for things people do that you appreciate, particularly those hidden right in front of you. When you see them, acknowledge them verbally or non-verbally. Then pay attention to any evidence of any appreciative circle rippling back to you.

Questions:

- What do you notice at home/school/work that you appreciate?

- What do you notice about your colleagues and friends that you appreciate?

- When you notice an appreciative circle rippling back to you, what effect does this have on you?

(Adapted from Hackett 2005, p.83)

Finding strengths in people who are socially isolated

Not everyone has a support network of friends or relatives who can give them feedback about their strengths, especially where their violence has resulted in them being removed from their homes; or where the violence is extreme, other people's views are not seen as important. In these situations, you can either look into the person's past or create an imaginary audience for the present. In the former instance a useful question is, 'What is the hardest thing you have ever done?' This leads on to the conversation about personal qualities such as persistence, resilience and courage. Alternatively, you may ask, 'What have you done that made you proud?' This question leads to a conversation about skills and abilities. You can also create an imaginary audience by asking questions such as, 'Suppose you had a goldfish in your sitting room. It has become very bored with swimming round and round the bowl, so has taken to studying you. What good things will it have noticed about you that no one else has noticed?' This question invites the person to discuss very small strengths and resources, but size doesn't matter in solution focused work; like building a snowman, the hardest bit is forming the tiny core. Even if the person can't think of anything the goldfish notices when first asked, the goldfish is still there watching out for qualities that can be developed and used in the solution.

PRACTICE ACTIVITY 5.4 (SPARKLING MOMENTS)

This is an idea developed by BRIEF[1] which, in turn, is based on ideas from narrative therapy.[2]

- Think of a time when you were at your best, when you felt 'sparkling'. Describe it briefly.

- What was it in particular about the moment which caused it to stand out?

- What are you most pleased to remember about yourself at that moment?

- What else were you pleased to notice? What else? What else?

---

1   E-mail address: info@brief.org.uk
2   Website: www.dulwichcentre.com.au

- If these qualities were to play a bigger part in your life, who would be the first to notice?

- What would they see?

- What difference would that make?

More questions include the following:

- What do you like about being a parent? What have you learned from this?

- How do you usually solve problems?

- What do you do to cope in times of stress?

- Who would you turn to for help in dealing with problems?

- How is it that, faced with all this, you have been determined to do the best you can for your children?

- How did you find the courage to plead guilty?

- What gave you the strength to...?

- When was your last success? How did that go? What was your role in that success?

- Suppose you were to compliment yourself on your effort. What would you say?

- What qualities and skills does this success show that you have?

- When did you become aware that you have these qualities?

- When did other people become aware that you have these qualities?

- In what situations are these qualities most noticeable?

- How could you use these qualities more?

- What is already going well and doesn't need to change?

- How do you most enjoy spending your time?

- What do you do better than others?

- What is easy for you that others probably find difficult?

- What activities do you find relaxing?

- Have you ever conquered a bad habit? How did you do that?

- What qualities do you value in others?

- We all have something unique to offer. What is it that you have to offer?

- What is or was your best subject at school?

- What positive things would your teacher say about you?

- What is your speciality at work?

- In what area do others consult you?

- Which of your qualities and abilities are most valued by people at work?

- What is the most important quality you should remember you have when you are under pressure?

- Which people in your life have been supportive of you?

- What positive influences did these people have on you?

- What did you learn from them?

- What did you value about them?

(Adapted from Turnell and Edwards 1999; Bannink 2010; and Sharry *et al.* 2012)

Strengths that build safety

The range of strengths and resources that people may have is very specific to the person, depending on their skills and situation. These strengths may be about others; for example, we might be impressed that there is someone in their family whom they respect and who can help them develop a violence-free future. Some of the questions we may want to ask people, that complement those in the exception-finding of Chapter 3, include:

- Is there anything you have done of which you are particularly proud?

- Is there something that you really tried hard to do that went well?

- At what are you good?

- At what would your family/friends say you are good?

We may want to ask more-focused questions that encourage ideas about solutions that are specific to violence:

- What is a good example of when you have taken responsibility?

- How have you shown that you can be respectful to others?

- How did you go about developing your friendships?

- What skills do you have in 'getting on' in your family?

- How did you sort out a problem with your friends in a non-violent way?

- How did you get the job and manage to get on in your workplace?

- Who of your friends is the one who talks you out of being violent? How does she or he do this?

- Is there any time you have encouraged others not to be violent? How did you do this?

Bateman and Milner (2015, p.73), in their work with children and young people who have sexually concerning behaviour, suggest that strengths-searching questions can be used with the families involved to help them develop safety. This recognises that the families have a central role to play in preventing further abuse and helps them to be involved in the process rather than simply being told by professionals how to manage the problem behaviour. These questions may include:

- Can you tell me something about your daughter that makes you proud as parents?

- How have you managed to carry on despite the recent upset and difficulties?

- What does this say about you as a family?

- What does it say about your strengths?

- What strengths would you identify as standing out in your family?

- Did you know that about yourself/your family?

- Can you tell me about other times where you have faced difficulties and specifically what you did which helped you to keep going?

- What ideas do you have about how these strengths and experiences can help you now?

PRACTICE ACTIVITY 5.5

We met Charles in Chapter 1, where he was physically and verbally bullying colleagues at work. Charles had worked as a social worker previously and had dealt with some very difficult cases where violence was a concern.

- Presuming that everyone has some strengths, what questions would you want to ask Charles to elicit these strengths?

- Speculating about what answers might be given, how might his strengths be used to find solutions to his violence?

When strengths or resources have been identified, the key issue in working with violence is how they can be used to build safety. In themselves, strengths are not necessarily indicators of safety; it is whether they have the potential to be used to develop *future* safety. Simply because someone is good at a range of activities or has positive qualities does not necessarily mean that this outweighs or balances their problematic behaviour.

PRACTICE EXAMPLE 5.5

Charles and his solution focused counsellor identified several strengths and skills that he had developed during his time as a social worker. These strengths and skills included tenacity, good judgement, the skills to persuade 'difficult' families, good relationships with the police and excellent case recording. Charles struggled to see how these strengths and skills could be used to develop safety for his colleagues and said that he wasn't motivated to change. The counsellor was unable to recommend a return to work on the basis that Charles was not yet ready to take appropriate responsibility for changing his behaviour and therefore there was not enough safety to prevent the behaviour from reoccurring.

We are interested in people's strengths and resources as they indicate a foundation on which change can be built. In themselves, personal qualities, skills and resources are not the same as safety; they are to be developed into tangible and measurable safety so that you not only identify and acknowledge a person's strengths and resources, you also follow up with questions such as:

- How did you do that?
- Did you know that about yourself?
- Can you do more of it?

Chapter 6

Scaling Safety and Progress

Scaling questions

Scaling questions enable people to identify where they are in relation to their problem or goal at that time, recognise how they got to that point, set realistic and achievable goals in both the short and long term, and measure their progress in realising these goals. They also identify a person's capacity, willingness and confidence to change. Most people are familiar with the 1–10 pain scale asked by medical staff. In these cases the actual numbers mean something tangible and, depending on the answer, differing levels of pain relief are administered. In solution focused practice the numbers mean nothing, except to each individual person; one person's 9 might be another person's 4. They are simply a way of asking a person about their perceptions of the situation and beginning a dialogue about how that situation can be improved. If you ask a person 'On a scale of 0–10, with 0 meaning [victim's name] is not at all safe with you and 10 meaning [victim's name] is completely safe, where would you put yourself at this moment?', the number selected has meaning only for that person. The person who has been on the receiving end of the violence may well give a different number when asked to rate their feelings of safety, and the worker's rating may be different from both of these numbers.

PRACTICE EXAMPLE 6.1

Stuart assessed Sally's safety from 'being hit' as high 'because it doesn't happen that often'. He was shocked when she assessed her safety as very low but he was able then to talk about how the unpredictability of his violence was more frightening than a 'regular beating' would have been:

> I can remember ducking every time my dad came near...he didn't hit us that much but we never knew when it was coming...but I must have ducked twenty times a day.

(Milner and Jessop, 2003 p.134)

What scaling questions do is 'create a dialogue that automatically assumes a *continuum* from danger to safety' (Turnell and Edwards 1999, p.74). With creativity about how they are presented, they can be used with people of all ages and ability. They are especially useful when working with risky situations, which are hard to quantify, as they facilitate the measurement of safety. They also allow the people harmed to have a voice in the assessment. Furthermore, people respond well to them as it is much less threatening to be talking about what they are doing to make their lives better rather than dwelling on past sins. As one man said to us, 'Ah, I get it. It's better to be ploughing fresh fields than digging up bones in the graveyard'.

PRACTICE ACTIVITY 6.1

Consider the last piece of work you undertook with a user of your service.

- On a scale of 0–10, where 0 is the worst work you could have done and 10 is the very best, where would you rate this piece of work?

- What would you have been doing differently if you had been able to rate it one point higher?

- How would the user of your service know you were doing it at the higher number?

- How would your supervisor know that you were doing it at the higher number?

- What will you be doing differently to achieve the higher number next time?

(Myers 2007, p.63)

Scaled questions for safety goal setting

People who have harmed others are not usually keen to talk about it; here scaled questions about well-being are useful ways of agreeing on goals. A basic solution focused question is: 'Suppose we have a scale of 0–100, with 100 being the best person you could be. Where on this scale would you place yourself right now?' We have never known anyone place themselves at 100, so wherever people place themselves, you have the beginnings of a conversation about change. Some follow-up questions include:

- On a scale of 1–10, how satisfied are you with your score?

- Where on the scale would you prefer to be?

- When you are one point higher on the best-person-you-can-be scale, what will you be doing differently?

- Where do you think [victim, referrer] would put you on this scale?

- What will you be doing differently that will tell that person you are higher on the scale?

- What help will you need to get a point higher?

Not everyone wants to move up smoothly a point at a time; asking about moving one point higher is merely to begin talking about movement. Some people are okay with where they are right now because it's the best they can do in difficult circumstances. Some want to take big steps, especially as hope rises once small steps have been achieved. Moreover, the very occasional person doesn't want to move at all; here you know very clearly that the situation is dangerous.

We also find it useful to ask a similar question about happiness: 'Suppose we have a happiness scale with 0 being life couldn't get worse and 100 is life couldn't get better, where on this scale would you place yourself today?' We have had people go off the bottom end of the scale and it is not uncommon for people who are violent to be quite low in spirit as they hear nothing but negative comments about their behaviour. The same follow-up questions are then asked to help the person work out a doable safety goal with the addition of questions such as:

- What does happiness look like to you?

- As well as being smiley, what else will you be doing when you are happier?

- What would you be doing that would make me realise that you are happier?

- Would anyone else notice that you are happier?

Like all solution focused questions, it's important not to rush your questions, giving the person plenty of time to think – and begin thinking deeply. One of the best compliments we have had was from a man who replied to his probation officer's comment that attending our programme sounded like a soft option: 'Nah…she makes me think'. The thinking required to engage fully in the solution focused process is profound, and often tiring, so we not infrequently comment on this with questions such as:

- You've worked hard today; what is the pace like for you?

- Could we have gone a little slower than today? Quicker?

- After all of today's hard work, how are you going to treat yourself this evening?

These sorts of questions are important not only because we have a duty of care but also because we want the person to begin looking at how they do self-care as well as how they care for others. This is also true of people who have been living with violence over a period of time, particularly women who tend to try to manage everyone's emotions to the detriment of their own well-being and ability to come to a decision about their own goals. Here we would ask questions such as:

- Suppose we have a responsibility scale where 0 is you take no responsibility and 10 is you take all the responsibility for what happens in your family. Where on this scale would you place yourself?

- On a scale of 0–10, how achievable do you think your score is?

- On a scale of 0–10, what do you think would be a reasonable score in the circumstance in which you are living?

- On a scale of 0–10, where 0 is not at all safe and 10 is completely safe, how safe are you right now?

Not all the questions go from 0 to 10 in safety assessment; some are reversed as they make more sense that way round. It is important to remember which way round you ask your scales, and it can help if you draw the scale on a piece of paper with the 'meanings' written at each end. Not only are these drawings useful for your records, but they are also a visual reminder of the person's progress at later sessions.

PRACTICE EXAMPLE 6.2

Asma married against her parents' wishes, and her own doubts, but she believed her husband would change once he learned to trust in her love for him. In the early stages of the relationship, he was physically abusive, and this has escalated since the birth of their baby 18 months ago. He knocks her to the ground and sits on her chest, pulling her hair, saying he will not get off until she stops crying. When she stops crying, he forces her to have sex – she agrees to this because she knows the violence will then stop for a week or so – and he tells her that he loves her and that she enjoys sex with him. His sexual violence is the part of his behaviour she loathes most. She is desperate to leave him but has not been able to do this yet as he is a good father to their child and looks after him while she works and studies part-time, he owns their house and he has threatened to follow her anywhere she goes. Her parents are supportive and would give her a home, but she doesn't want to 'be a child again'. She did live in a refuge for a short while but was unhappy there.

PRACTICE ACTIVITY 6.2

Devise five scaled safety questions you could ask that might help Asma develop a personal goal that is reasonable and achievable.

Questions for assessing safety

Using a 0- to 10-point scale, we ask the person who has done harm how safe they rate the person and/or people they have harmed and compare this other person's ratings:

- On a scale of 0–10, where 0 means [the person harmed] is not at all safe from you and 10 means they are completely safe, where do you place yourself right now?

- On a scale of 0–10, where 0 means you feel not at all safe from [the person who has harmed] and 10 is you feel completely safe, where do you place yourself right now?

- Are these scores higher or lower than previously?

- [Where they are higher] What have you done differently to increase the safety rating?

- Where would [the person who is complaining about the violent person] put you on this scale?

- What will you be doing differently when [the harmed person] feels safer?

- What will [the person who has harmed you] be doing differently when you feel safer?

- [Where the harmful person has been separated from family or school] What will you be doing differently that would convince [your mum, your head teacher, your social worker, the judge] that you are safe to [go home, back to school, have contact with your children]?

PRACTICE EXAMPLE 6.3

Shannon and Brendan, who both have mild learning difficulties, have been together for 5 years, having met originally at school. Their relationship has been characterised by domestic violence with Shannon saying that Brendan going on about her not doing enough in the house winds her up until she snaps and hits him. She describes herself as 'like the Incredible Hulk, only not green'. Brendan is easily frustrated by officialdom and can be verbally aggressive when professionals tell him what to do. They have an 11-month-old baby, Ruby, who has been in care since she was 5 months old following a report from the health visitor that the parents were feeding the child unsuitable food, such as fizzy drinks and potato crisps. The social worker is considering adoption on the grounds of Brendan's aggressiveness and non-compliance with the care plan (he drove Shannon to see her father in another town despite having neither driving licence nor insurance), Shannon's lack of effort at initiating stimulating play with Ruby in contact sessions and her non-compliance with a diet plan to help her lose weight.

Judith: Suppose I have a parenting scale where 0 is the worst parent you could be and 10 is the very best parent. Where would you put yourself on this scale?

Shannon: About five.

Brendan: About there (indicates 90% on the drawn scale). Because no one's perfect, are they? I'd say about three quarters that way (points toward 10).

Judith: Where do you think your social worker would put you on this scale?

They look at each other, taking their time with the question.

Shannon (dejectedly): Zero.

Brendan: Yeah, zero. She told us she's had four kids adopted this year and Ruby's going to be next.

Judith: Oh, dear! Can you think of anything you could do differently that would get her to put you a bit higher up the scale?

Shannon: I've tried, but she says I don't play with Ruby enough. I do but they are always watching you and writing stuff down. It makes me feel awkward.

Brendan: We know now not to feed Ruby crisps and things like that, but the social worker has made up her mind.

Judith: What can you do to show her that you've learned how to feed a baby properly?

Shannon: It's hard because we're a bit backward. No, I mean we've got... (looking to Brendan) What's it called?

Brendan: Learning disability.

Shannon: Yeah, learning disability...only it's mild. I *want* to learn how to look after Ruby better, but they just tell me what I'm doing wrong. Like the playing with her. I'd like some help to choose some right toys for her.

Brendan: We've no chance. They've made up their mind.

Usually the person who feels unsafe will not give a rating way below that of the violent person, although sometimes they do. This doesn't matter because however close the scores are, there is still room for discussion about what needs to be different to achieve congruence and safety. Having a discussion about differences in safety ratings aids tangible and achievable safety planning and broadens strategies for dealing with potential flashpoints; for example: 'Walking out when you feel angry works for you, but this leaves other people behind who are wondering when you are coming back and what you will be like when you come back. What can you do differently before you return that will make everyone feel safe – and looking forward to your return?' Neil was astonished when his partner, Joshua, said that he would feel safer when Neil stopped saying horrible things which hurt more than the beatings. Neil talked about how he thought it would take time before the nastiness at the back of his mind would go away, so 'nastiness' was externalised as an oppressive enemy. He was asked if it suited him to have 'nastiness' ruling his life, and what would he be doing differently when he had 'niceness' at the back of his mind.

There is no reason why children should not be involved in safety scaling. When working with families or groups, it helps to have a flip chart and draw a number of scales such as temper control, frustration, shouting, self-calming, consideration, respect and so forth, and any scales which are relevant to the current situation. We also find it helps to ask the most powerful person to write up people's scores as this takes them out of the situation somewhat and helps them listen. With families or small groups, you can ask circular scaled questions in which you hand out pieces of paper and pencils and ask each person to write their scores but not let anyone see what they are writing. Then you ask people to guess what they think another person wrote. However serious the violence, this can often turn out to be a session that is filled with laughter and one where the younger members' creativity means that they start creating more scales for their parents to answer. One large family all came together because the mother wanted to hear what the father was saying in his sessions, and as there was no one else to look after the children, they came too. Mostly they played but soon became interested in the scales and devised a 'dad's grumpiness' scale. Their mother laughed as they gave him low scores, but she was not so pleased when they promptly drew a 'mum's grumpiness' scale on the flip chart. She didn't score well either, but violence is often complicated by a number of factors. With a large group, such as a school classroom tackling a bullying issue, scaling questions can be used as part of a safe classroom project. Possible questions include:

- What makes a safe classroom?

- On a scale of 0–10, where 0 is you feel completely safe and 10 is you don't feel at all safe, how safe do you feel in this classroom?

- What will be happening differently when you feel one point safer?

- What will you be doing differently when you feel one point safer?

- What is happening now that makes the classroom safe?

- Of what do you need to do more to build on the safety that is already happening?

PRACTICE ACTIVITY 6.3

With a group of colleagues, think of a hobby or sport you currently enjoy and at which you would like to be better. Set out cards with 0–10 on the floor with 0 meaning you are performing as badly as you can imagine and 10 meaning you are consistently performing at your personal peak. Place yourself on the scale and explore with the person nearest to you the following questions:

- How did you get to this point?

- What does 10 represent?

- Where would you like to be?

- What do you need to do to get to that point?

- What help do you require?

- Who would be best placed to help you?

- What is a reasonable time scale for this to happen?

(Adapted from Milner and Bateman 2011, pp.116–117)

Questions that assess likelihood of change

Although it is important for people who have been violent to take responsibility for the safety of others, you can set the scene for motivation to change to be increased. Motivation has at least three components – willingness to change, confidence to change and capacity to change – so it is important to work out which aspect of motivation needs strengthening most. All too often, workers focus on capacity, giving out information when the person knows exactly what needs to be done to change but lacks either willingness or confidence to do so. The three basic questions are:

- If 0 means you can't be bothered and 10 means you will do anything it takes, where are you on this scale?

- If 10 means you are completely confident that you can reach your goal and 0 means you have no confidence at all, where are you on this scale?

- If 10 means you know exactly what you need to do to achieve your goal and 0 means you have no idea how to start, where are you on this scale?

These questions are then followed up with:

- How satisfied are you with this score?

- Where on this scale would you like to be?

- Are there times when you have been higher on this scale?

- What were you doing differently then?

- What have you forgotten to do that was working for you last time?

- [Where the score is high] From where does this willingness to work hard come? How did you do that?

- [Where the score is low] How did you manage to reach 2? How come it's not 0 or 1? What would 3 look like? What are your chances of getting one point higher?

- When you are one point higher, what will you be doing differently?

- What will other people notice about you that is different?

Scaled questions are also useful where there is lack of respect for other people:

- If 10 means that you have all possible respect for [person's name] and 0 means you have no respect, where would you say you are right now?

- Why is it not less?

- What mark would you like to reach in the future since this person has influence on your life?

- What is already working in the right direction?

- What would be the next step or sign of progress?

PRACTICE ACTIVITY 6.4

Reread the Shannon and Brendan case (i.e. Practice example 6.3).

- Do you think they lack willingness, confidence or capacity?
- Make a list of 10 possible questions you could ask them that would encourage constructive action on the part of these parents.
- Make a list of 10 possible questions you could ask their social worker.

PRACTICE ACTIVITY 6.5

Daniel has served a short prison term for sexual intercourse with a 15-year-old. He desperately wants to have contact with his two young children but only rated himself at 6 on the willingness scale because 'I'll do anything it takes, but when I get depressed, I sneak about and avoid the situation'.

- Devise five follow-up questions that are aimed at helping him handle his depression better and increase his motivation.

(Adapted from Milner 2008)

Assessing progress

The most commonly used scaled question asked to assess progress is: 'If 0 is where you were last time we talked and 10 is your problem is completely solved, where are you on this scale today?' This is followed by 'How satisfied are you with your score?' and then 'How did you do it?' Alternatively, you could ask, 'You rated [victim's] safety at 7 last time we talked. Where do you rate their safety today?' As before, the numbers don't actually mean anything; they are simply a means by which you can talk about the changes needing to be made, how they are to be accomplished and what the person has done differently. It is in the details that you are able to measure the presence of safety. Progress is rarely smooth; some people return for a second session with the problem entirely solved, others may be defensive because they have not made their desired progress.

PRACTICE EXAMPLE 6.4

Sophie hit her partner, argued constantly and rang him obsessively when he was at work, so he left her, taking their toddler, Elle, with him. Sophie had Elle to stay most weekends but didn't feel that these visits went well. She was continuing to harass David with constant text messages, although she was desperate to prove to him that her violence would stop. On a scale where 0 means she has no control over her behaviour and 10 means she has complete control, Sophie rated herself at 6. She could not think what she could do to move up a point as there was a great deal of compulsion in her thoughts and behaviour, so she was asked the miracle question to which she was able to respond about how she would 'have sorted out herself, her house and her business'. She thought this would take a month to accomplish but rang to cancel her appointment, rescheduling for a month later.

Sophie rated her self-control at 9 on her second appointment. She described how she started by repairing and then painting her house. She did a lot of thinking while painting, devising a plan of action which was successful over all areas of her life, and accomplished the following:

- She paid off her business debts and acquired new premises.

- She took Elle shopping to choose paint and furnishings for her bedroom. She described how rewarding she found this and how much her relationship with Elle had improved.

- She had a long-overdue argument with her mother during which she told her she wasn't going to listen to her mother's constant put-downs any more.

- She stopped her occasional drug use.

- She refrained from constantly texting David. As a result, their relationship was improving and they were visiting each other for meals.

Painting her house had been a big job, giving Sophie time to reflect on her life and develop patience. She felt that becoming more patient was her most important achievement: 'Before, everything had to be *now*. Now it can wait. I'm more chilled. It feels good'.

When people report that they have changed but cannot give any details, you can safely assume that there has been no change and take whatever steps are necessary for other people's safety. Mike reported that his partner, Amy, was now at 10 on the 'How safe is Amy?' scale but couldn't say what he had done differently other than describe driving mindlessly across the country until his car broke down and having some sort of epiphany. He said he was a changed man but could not explain in what way, so Amy was assessed as unsafe. Keeping people safe in such dangerous situations is rarely as simple as leaving the person who has harmed them. Often there is an emotional tie that prevents them from making the break. Here we ask safety questions such as:

- How do know you will be all right?

- What can you do, and what can I do, to help me understand that you will be all right?

- What are the things that make you know you are going to be all right?

- Could you tell me about these things? I might feel a whole lot safer about it all if I knew these things.

- [For people in the home with a dangerous partner who has locked them in previously] Have you got a safety pack in case you need to get out quickly? Do you keep a door key on your person at all times? Have got a spare set of car keys somewhere safe for emergencies? Do you keep the car filled up with fuel? Have you got an emergency fund of money you can access?

- [For young people at risk when out socially] Do you pre-book a taxi before you go out? Do you stick together when you go out? Do you make sure your mobile phone is topped up? Do you ask a mate to come with you when you go to the toilet? Do you agree that one of you will stay sober each time you go out?

- [For children or vulnerable elderly people living with a relative who denies being violent toward them] Who can you contact if you don't feel safe? Have you got a mobile phone? Is that person's number in your phone? Do you have a secret sign, such as moving an ornament, that would alert people to the fact that you don't feel safe?

PRACTICE ACTIVITY 6.6

Devise a list of safety questions you might ask either:

- a group of young people at risk of being bullied on the way home from school by older youths; or

- an elderly person whom you suspect is being hit by their carer but who doesn't want their carer to be removed.

For people who decide to part from a violent partner or relative, questions need to be asked about how this can be achieved safely. A sudden flight without belongings or someone to run to is likely to result in a return to the 'devil you know'. Questions would include those about a safety pack listed above and:

- On a scale of 0–10, where 0 means you have no chance of getting out of the situation and 10 means you are completely confident that your escape plans will work, where are you on this scale right now?

- Have you decided where you will go?

- Who can you depend on to help you?

- Are there any treasured belongings you don't want to leave behind?

PRACTICE EXAMPLE 6.5

Session notes
Name: Amy

Problem
Amy is someone who always gives 100% when she loves someone. Sadly, Mike, with whom she has lived for 4 years, took advantage of her love: he had an affair, was controlling and expected her to do all the cleaning and cooking (and looking after his two kids). Then he got violent: he not only hit Amy and abused her verbally, but he also terrified her when he locked her in the house and threatened to slit her throat with a knife he had ready. Despite all this, he thinks she will come back to him because he still loves her.

Amy doesn't think much of the way he 'loves' her; in fact, she doesn't want to be loved by him at all. She wants to be happy and comfortable, not to live in fear, and never to see him again. When this happens, she will be in her flat, bouncing out of bed for a cup of tea. Then she will put on some make-up, do her hair really nice, wear an attractive trouser suit (maybe white because she looks good in this) and spend the day with her sister. They might call to see their father at the working men's club (WMC). They will be talking about how they enjoy their freedom.

Exceptions/progress

- It took a few goes but Amy got herself away from Mike's violence and started to keep herself safe.

- Sleeping has been hard for Amy, mainly because she has dreams about the children. She misses the children dreadfully but has an idea how to handle this.

- There is still a nervous part to Amy when she's out. She gets anxious about meeting Mike's family in town because half of them blame her. She isn't letting this stop her going out, though.

- Amy didn't have a happy childhood because of what her father did to her mother, but she is on good terms with all her family and is using their support to help her through this bad time.

Thoughts on solutions

- Amy escaped Mike's violence by going to her mother's home, then across the road to a neighbour, and hedge hopping to get to a friend Mike didn't know. Then she got in touch with Angela at the domestic-violence forum. Angela got her a flat and arranged for her to have counselling. She will also arrange for Amy to have an extra lock, an alarm and a security light. All these things help Amy keep safe.

- Amy got some sleeping pills from her general practitioner (GP) to help with the sleeping and takes them sensibly. She intends to keep a diary for the children about how much she misses them so they can have it later in life. She isn't ready yet to do this, but she thinks it will happen soon.

- When Amy goes out, she takes care to do this in daylight. In the flat, she only puts lights on in the rooms with curtains and listens to her music while she works. This makes her feel good because she knows she can do this when she is living there and soaking in the bath getting ready to go out and have a leisurely day with her sister. Being in the flat really helps Amy feel optimistic about her life and freedom. She had the good sense to get a taxi back.

- Her mother helped Amy by always telling the family to stick together and tell the truth. Amy feels good now that she isn't having to tell lies about her life. She sees her dad too, at the WMC, and loves him now that he's a mellow old man. She talks to all the older men at the club (a safe place for her because Mike is banned), and it helped her sort out her feelings and actions when she advised a man how to escape being abused by his wife.

Homework

- More of the same – it's working! Every time Amy does something in the flat, it becomes safer and she can see how her life will be. She will be in the flat, having lots of company.

- She will take even more safety precautions – Mike is really dangerous. She will carry a small can of hairspray in her handbag, and when she is in the flat, she will ring for help if she needs it.

Sometimes you suspect that the details of 'how they did it' are not real, that the person is making them up. This actually doesn't matter a great deal as they are rehearsing how to go about making changes in their behaviour. It means that you remain cautious and wait for the real details to emerge.

In most cases you can check on progress by consulting other people in the situation, repeating your earlier questions about how safe they feel right now. These people include not only those who were harmed but also parents, teachers, social workers and so forth. Where they report increased levels of safety, again you ask for details of what is happening differently that has increased safety. For example, one woman described an argument starting but 'instead of him getting that *face* on, he said, "I'm going for a bath. Can we talk about this later?" And we did and it went all right'. The man is then asked how he did this and his account is checked against the reports of others in the situation. At all times a focus on safety is maintained, checking that there is progress toward the agreed outcomes and whether the progress is quick enough, updating the safety plan accordingly.

PRACTICE EXAMPLE 6.6

Table 6.1a Safe-care plan for Latrell (age 14 years) and Kiara (age 9 years); parents are Devon and Jennifer

Concerns (historic, recent and current)	Evidence of safety	What safety will look like
When the parents lived together, the children witnessed them fighting each other (historic).	The children report that there has been no physical fighting since their parents separated.[a]	The parents will be cooperating with each other.
The parents were dishonest with social workers about the degree of their separation (historic).	Initially the parents kept in touch by text, but this ceased when Jennifer deliberately broke her phone and stopped answering the door.[b]	The parents will have sufficient contact with each other to ensure their children's well-being and maintain relationships with extended family members.
Latrell was beginning to challenge authority at school (historic).	Latrell recognises that he has an 'attitude' and is working on being more respectful. His 'attitude' is affected by his mood, so he would benefit from work on handling his emotional states.[a]	Latrell will be attending school and getting on with his teachers. His homework will be done on time and he will be making academic progress.
Devon became increasingly frustrated with Latrell's behaviour, resulting in Latrell asking to come into care because he was afraid of him (recent).	Devon recognises that how he responded to Latrell didn't work, so he is negotiating more. Jennifer reported that Devon's attitude is indeed different. Latrell reports that Devon talks more and says when he's unhappy with Latrell's behaviour in a calm way. Kiara reports that Devon isn't shouting as much and being much more calm.[a]	Devon will have developed other ways of responding to Latrell's challenging behaviour (what Jennifer refers to as 'having his funny head on').

Concerns (historic, recent and current)	Evidence of safety	What safety will look like
Social workers consider that Kiara is at risk of chastisement at the hands of Devon when she becomes older and more challenging of his authority (recent).	Kiara says that she is not frightened of Devon, and this is evidenced by her giving him a 'yellow card' when she thought his 'bantering' was too much. My observations of Kiara with Devon are that she is cheekily playful with him. Jennifer reports that Kiara twists Devon round her little finger and is pretty spoiled.[a]	Kiara will be lively, cheerful and confident when she is in Devon's company.
Jennifer's lifestyle continues to be chaotic, with missed contacts and evidence of drinking and substance misuse (recent).	Until the phone-smashing episode, Jennifer was keeping all her appointments. Since then, she has missed a Saturday contact with Kiara.[b]	Jennifer will be attending all appointments, making sure her mobile phone is working and ringing up if she has a sound reason for missing an appointment.
Both parents continue to misuse substances and this has an effect on Latrell's substance misuse (current).	Jennifer made an appointment to attend the substance misuse centre, but she didn't keep it. Devon uses substances only when the children are sleeping over with relatives on Saturdays.[c]	The parents will be working to reduce their substance misuse.
The parents do not communicate constructively (current).	The parents have the capacity to communicate constructively: they attended family meetings, went together to Kiara's school open day and made arrangements by text. All this stopped after Jennifer smashed her phone.[c]	The parents will be communicating constructively and peacefully with each other and professionals.
Devon lacks appropriate parenting skills to handle Latrell's challenging behaviour (current).	Devon is developing more effective ways of handling Latrell but would probably benefit from further assistance.[a]	Devon will have developed appropriate ways of responding to Latrell's challenging behaviour.

When Jennifer has a low mood, she withdraws and becomes unreliable (current).	Jennifer made a good start to handling her low moods by visiting her GP who arranged for her to be assessed by a certified psychiatric nurse, who has put her on the waiting list for therapy.[c] However, she has not informed the social worker of changes to her mobile number. Devon returned her SIM card from the broken mobile via Latrell, but the phone remains switched off. She isn't answering the door.[b]	Jennifer will be taking good care of her physical and mental health. She will be reliable and able to ask for help when necessary.

Although no colours are shown here, we colour code progress as developing safety, potential safety and no safety to distinguish between different levels of safety. Workers say that indicating no safety in red is really helpful in maintaining the focus on the children. According to our codes, blue (represented here as superscript 'a') indicates developing safety, green (represented here as superscript 'c') indicates potential safety and red (represented here as superscript 'b') indicates no safety.

Table 6.1b Goals of everyone involved

Children's goals	Parents' goals	Social Care's goals
Latrell wants to live with Jennifer (first choice) but otherwise with Devon. He misses Kiara and wants to spend lots more time with her. Kiara would like everyone to be back living together but, failing that, she would like to live with Devon and spend a lot more time with Jennifer and Latrell.	Devon would like to be able to work with Jennifer and is very disappointed that she isn't putting Latrell first. Should Jennifer not be able to communicate more reliably with Devon, he would like Latrell to live with him so that the children will be together, and he will know where Latrell is each evening.	Social workers would like Devon to agree to Latrell being accommodated, and subject to a supervision order, while a family support plan is established so that he can live with Devon.
	Jennifer's goals are not known at the moment.	
Both kids want their parents to stop arguing and solve their problems.	See above.	Social workers hope Devon can support the children more constructively when they are let down by Jennifer.
Both kids want to be involved in discussions with social workers and their parents (i.e. treated as a family unit).	Devon is happy with the referral to the parenting support unit. Jennifer's views are unknown.	They want the parents to attend all school meetings.

Being creative

It doesn't have to be all about 0–10. You can devise a scale to meet each situation, and while some people prefer a numbered scale, others respond well to a drawing of the problem to be defeated or a scale using other people as examples. When people talk about their inability to control their violence because it comes on suddenly, often described as a red mist descending, we ask for more detail about whatever it is that is controlling them. Is it temper, impatience, frustration, fury and so forth? We also ask what colour it is and where are the first signs of it appearing in the body, and does it go fists, mouth or feet? Then we construct scales that are relevant to it, such as if 0 is you have no control over red raging bull and 10 is you have it on the ropes, where are you on this scale right now? Most people initially refer to red rage, but we find that tempers come in all colours, shapes and sizes. One man was so angry about his much younger partner's behaviour when working as bar staff in a local pub – wearing low-cut jeans that showed her underwear – that he would drive her home telling her what a beating she would get later and drive slowly at traffic lights so she would try to jump out of the car – at which point he would speed up, even if the lights were still red! It wasn't necessary to ask him what colour his anger was; his face was dark grey with fury and upset, so we asked him: 'If 0 is you are feeling really loving and caring toward your partner and 10 is you could definitely murder her, where are you on this scale right now?' His relief at being asked a question that reflected the magnitude of his anger was manifest and he was able to answer 9. He could not think of any way he could reduce this rating as he also suffered severe depression following high amphetamine use. His answers precipitated his partner into thinking more about her safety.

In child protection cases, we ask the parents whom they consider to be the best and worst fathers and mothers in the whole world and then use these people in scaling questions. Parents don't expect to be at either end of the scale, so this allows lots of room for questions about what they will be doing differently when they move up the scale. For violence in school, we ask, 'Who is the best behaved person in your class/year/school and who is the worst?' (This depends on the severity of the violence as they may well be the worst behaved in their class but rarely in the whole school.) This is followed up by, 'Where on this scale do you place yourself right now, and where on this scale would you like to be?' We also ask, 'Which kid in your class can get away with murder and which kid always gets caught? How do you think the kid who gets away with it does this? Would these things be useful to you, or would it be helpful to borrow his or her life for a day to see if it makes a difference?' With younger kids who are violent at home, we ask, 'If 0 is a devil and 10 is an angel, where are you on this scale today?' The strength in these questions is that they all reflect a continuum so are a relatively non-threatening way of talking about a serious problem. It is not unusual for people spontaneously to say what number they are at, especially where there has been significant improvement. Also, it doesn't have to be 0–10; adolescents often prefer a scale of 0–100 or 0–100,000, and young children seem to get on well with drawings of the problem or ladder scales. People with learning difficulties also like a creative approach which breaks the problem into small, tangible pieces. This also allows the person time to think. We've found that the slower we go, the quicker the progress.

PRACTICE EXAMPLE 6.7

Twelve-year-old Tim has Asperger's syndrome and mild learning difficulty. He is on the verge of being excluded from school following regular temper tantrums and sexually harassing girls. On a scale of 0 is the worst temper ever and 10 is completely calm, Tim rates himself at 5. He doesn't know what he would be doing if he was at 6, so he is asked to consult his helping team – his foster carer, Sally, and her granddaughter, Anna.

Tim: You mean like ask the audience?

Judith: Why not?

Tim: No, I'll phone a friend. (He puts his hand to his ear.) You'll have to do it too, Judith.

Judith: Okay. (She puts her hand to her ear.) Is that Sally? Hello. I have Tim here and he's answered all the questions so far, but he's got stuck on this one: What will he being doing differently when he gets to 6 on the temper-taming scale? You have 30 seconds starting from now.

Sally begins to answer but is distracted by Tim counting down the seconds loudly. Then Judith's mobile rings, distracting everyone.

Sally: I need more time to think.

Tim (picking up the mobile): We can use this.

Judith: Okay. I'll ring you. (She pretends to use a mobile.) Hello. Is that Tim's teacher? I have Tim here and he's answered all the questions so far, but he's stuck on this one: What will he be doing differently when he gets to 6 on the temper-taming scale?

Tim (as his teacher): He's a horror to work with. Let me see, he'll be sitting quietly, not moving around, keeping calm and not walking out of class.

Judith: Thank you. That is most helpful. (She puts down the imaginary mobile.) Well, you heard what your teacher said. Do you think you can do any of those things?

Tim: Yes.

Judith: Which one would be the easiest to start?

Tim: Not moving around.

Judith: How will you do that?

Tim: I knew you were going to ask me that! I'll just do it.

(Adapted from Milner and Bateman 2011, pp.125–126)

PRACTICE ACTIVITY 6.7

Think of a person with whom you are working but not making the progress you would like.

- Devise a scale that is appropriate for that person.

We find scaling to be one of the most useful and accessible tools in the solution focused kit. It is simple and straightforward, and most people can both use it and understand it. Unlike some other scales, such as a GP who may ask your pain scale and prescribe according to the rating, the actual score is relatively unimportant; what *is* useful is exploring the detail between the current score and what would be happening when it is different. This provides the space to talk about change. Safety becomes much more nuanced and detailed if we accept that it is on a continuum, rather than either/or, and this enables further clarity about what needs to change.

Chapter 7

Ending a Session

Deciding on tasks

Having listed concerns, agreed on goals and discovered strengths and exceptions, the next thing to do is decide how to go about the solution. Solution focused practitioners have devised a set of homework tasks which are developed with the person, who is invited to have a go or experiment with them and keep track of any difference that is made. Questions include:

- What homework would be most useful for you?

- Suppose you could do with a suggestion. What might it be?

- Suppose you wanted to give yourself a homework suggestion. What might it be?

(Adapted from Bannink 2010)

The invitation is a permissive one in that the person can change the task or do something else that occurs to them that might be more useful. Unlike cognitive behavioural approaches, there is no expectation that the task will be done or have a specific effect; it is merely a way of enabling people to note times when the problem isn't happening and changes that are beneficial. In many instances people report back that they had a 'better idea'.

Where a situation is vague, a *formula* (or standard) first-session (F1) task is given, asking people to list all those things that are happening in their life that they want to continue to happen. By listing what does *not* need to change, this exercise helps the clarification of appropriate goals. Sometimes people are so overwhelmed by their problems that they say they want to change everything and, here, it is useful to ask them to *take a step in a direction that will be good for them*. This helps them take a step toward taking responsibility for their future.

PRACTICE EXAMPLE 7.1

Amanda and Jake are in a cycle of action and reaction which they want to break. Anything can trigger an argument, and then Amanda gets into a rage. Her rage is red and it envelops her. Her heart starts pounding and her head feels as though it will explode. She screams and shouts as well as hits. It doesn't last long, mostly until one of them is on the floor. This is usually Amanda, but she has thrown a kettle of boiling water over Jake. It all goes back into place within minutes, but Amanda feels terrible afterwards.

Amanda has also suffered from severe depression following being taken for granted, feeling lonely and having difficulties with both her mother and daughter. Some days she feels like she can't get out of bed. Her goal is for the fighting to stop and to be working in a job that uses her skills and qualifications.

There are a number of exceptions:

- The fighting has only happened about eight times in 3 years of marriage. Other times, they just have petty bickering. They worked out that fighting is more likely to happen after they come back from watching a football match and they have been drinking. They are hyped up with the adrenalin flowing. They love their football, so they decided to take a flask of coffee to the next match. Other times, Amanda can stop the rage from erupting by doing breathing relaxation. This works when she has enough warning.

- Amanda had a vicious temper in high school, but she learned to control it then by walking away from situations.

- Depression, being taken for granted and her mother's put-downs have reduced Amanda's self-esteem, but she can think of a few good things about herself. The good things about herself that Amanda can remember are: she's a good listener, a good organiser, gregarious, intelligent and determined. (She got a City and Guilds certificate in landscape gardening part-time while bringing up her daughter single-handedly.) Her father would agree with all these things, plus that she is hard working.

- She has fought her way out of suicide mainly for Jake. The only thing she is doing for herself at the moment is her garden. She and Jake have completely landscaped it from scratch, and Amanda is growing all her plants from seed.

Amanda had clear ideas about how to control her rage but found dealing with her unhappiness and low self-esteem a 'mountain to climb'. She wanted to start with something small and achievable, so she was asked to take a step in a direction that was good for her. This is actually a very difficult task as it involves doing something that it sensibly selfish. Many people find it hard to accept that some degree of selfishness is necessary for emotional well-being. Amanda reported at the next meeting that she had decided a step in the right direction for her was to be focused and find serenity, so she had joined a yoga class. This helped control her mood. Being more in control of her mood had the effect of being able to express her feelings and preferences calmly, resulting in no rage – just one argument which didn't go further than agreeing to disagree. Jake had been making small life changes too but, combined, they were quite powerful, so his homework was to do more of the same.

As in the case of Jake, where there are clear exceptions and solutions are working, the person is simply asked how they did them and if they can *do more of them.* Solution focused practice can be described in a nutshell as:

- If it's not broken, don't fix it.

- If it's working, do more of it.

- If it's not working, do something different.

The skill of the worker in 'doing more of it' lies in their having identified the detail of the exceptions: how they did it; where they did it; when they did it; if anyone noticed; if anyone is needed to help; and so forth. 'Whatever the client is doing that is healthy and helpful and enhances better functioning in her real life, it is worth highlighting and repeating, even when it has no direct bearing on the problem' (Berg and Reuss 1998, p.51). *Doing something different* doesn't need to be so specific; the worker can simply appear puzzled that attempted solutions haven't worked so far, asking, 'What haven't you tried so far?' or saying, 'Think of one small thing you could do that's completely different from anything you've tried before'.

PRACTICE ACTIVITY 7.1

Make three lists, writing down:

1. what is going well in your life right now

2. what is just ticking over

3. what is not working.

Choose one item from list 1 and identify what you are doing that is successful. Can you do more of that in relation to one item in list 2? Choose one item from list 3 and plan to do something completely different. Tell a significant person in your life that you are undertaking an experiment (unspecified), so would they please study you and make a note of anything different they notice about you over the next week?

When a person is unable to recall an exception, a *pretend* task is suggested, for example, pretending to be calm one half of the week – or alternate days – and noticing what is different or what other people see is different. This helps to develop and identify possible exceptions that make a difference to the problem. It is also quite difficult to pretend a behaviour for any length of time without it becoming real.

PRACTICE ACTIVITY 7.2

Think of a work colleague with whom you find it difficult to work. Pretend all next week that you are getting on really well with this person. Tell a supportive colleague that you are undertaking an experiment (unspecified) and ask them to notice anything different about you over the next few days.

When working with children who have difficulty in controlling their temper, we add a twist, informing parents that their child is going to try an experiment on some days and we would like them to keep a note of anything different they notice about their child in the coming week or two, but we can't tell them which days are the experiment ones. This greatly increases temper control as children are only too pleased to have the opportunity to fool their parents.

Adding a coin toss to the task is helpful for people who are struggling to make a decision. Often the person who has been violent will be filled with remorse over their actions and promise never to do it again, so the injured person may be in two minds about whether to stay in the relationship or leave. In such an instance the worker could ask the person to toss a coin each evening – or morning, whichever suits the person best – with the following pretend task:

- If the coin comes up heads, pretend all day that you are staying with your partner, no matter how bad the situation gets. If the coin comes up tails, pretend all day that you are leaving, no matter how good things get.

This task has the advantage of taking out any thoughts about the pros and cons of the situation; it allows the person to focus on one possible solution at a time to see how it feels. It is not uncommon for people to toss the coin until they get the result that is already beginning to feel right for them. It also helps to personalise the task by asking questions about where the person might go for a holiday to celebrate when their solution has been found and then choose a coin that is relevant to the celebration.

PRACTICE EXAMPLE 7.2

Eleanor has been coping with the violence of her son, Bernard, for 25 years. He hasn't hit her for some time, but he shouts and bawls to get his own way. This frightens her. Sometimes he threatens her and tells her she's a poor mother and he hates her. This makes her feel guilty, and then she gives in. Mostly he wants money. She is scared and miserable and unhappy. Now that she is approaching pensionable age, she wants a quieter, more peaceful life, but she doesn't know how to go about it. She does not want to report Bernard to the police.

Eleanor couldn't think of any times she had been able to stand up to Bernard, so she was asked what would be different and how she would celebrate when the Bernard problem is solved. She said that she would have enough money from her pension lump sum to have a holiday in Ireland with her best friend. (This raised the very real problem that Bernard would threaten further when the money became due.) She agreed to toss an Irish coin each night. If it came up on the deer side, she would pretend all day that she will let Bernard bully her for the rest of her life – no matter how bad it gets. If it came up on harp side, she would pretend all day that she will do something about Bernard, no matter how nice he is.

By separating her mixed feelings of love and fear of Bernard, Eleanor was able to decide that she needed help. She enlisted the help of the local domestic-violence forum workers who set about changing her locks, fitting panic buttons and so forth. She rang

Bernard and told him that she would see him only in a public place accompanied by friends, and that she hoped he would attend an anger management group.

Where exceptions are spontaneous or the result of other people's efforts, that is, not deliberate on the violent person's part or seen as outside their control, the person can be asked to *predict* when spontaneous exceptions are going to happen. This is especially useful in work with people who have been sexually harmful. It has been found that they can improve their ability to predict this correctly with practice and, of course, when they can get a high proportion of predictions correct, the question is, 'Are the exceptions really spontaneous, or do you have some control? And if so, can you do more of it?' A prediction task also helps a person work out why some days are better than others. With a badly behaved pupil, a chart is often useful, whereas an adult can simply be asked to notice any differences.

PRACTICE EXAMPLE 7.3

Kayla has told Logan that she will not come back to him until he controls his terrible temper. He says it is worse when he has been drinking, but he still loses his temper when sober. He can control how far it goes when he is sober, but he finds this hard to do when he has been drinking. It is like a mini explosion, a mist that erupts after frustration sets in. The explosion has progressed from pushing Kayla away to slapping and kicking. After the explosion, he calms down right away. He has had the temper for a long time, although his fuse was longer when he was younger. He is not sure where it came from or how it got worse.

Logan can spot the warning signs when he is sober, so he has controlled his drinking. If he drinks in the house, he gets one bottle of wine instead of two or a four-pack to share instead of drinking one each. This is important as one helpful thing Logan does when he loses his temper is to jump into the car for a short drive. He also suffers from road rage but handles this when he is driving his work van by swearing or giving a blast on the horn.

He has started doing self-calming by giving himself the space to do so and telling himself to calm down, it's not worth losing his temper. This works when he can remember to do it.

Even though Logan's temper has got worse in some ways, he takes responsibility for the harm he has done Kayla and has learned a lot of ways of controlling his temper. He still struggles with frustration arising from not getting his own way – like needing to win – and responding badly to a put-down, although some days are better than others. He's pretty sure that the bad days are those where he has a pressurised day at work, but he's not sure what is different on better days.

To help Logan work out how he copes with some days and not others, he was asked to do a prediction experiment: keep a prediction chart of good days and bad days to see what is happening on bad days to wind him up and if he is right about which days will be which. He was also to do more of the same things that are working for him already.

Logan reported significant progress over the next two sessions and was accompanied by Kayla on his fourth (and final) session. They had been talking on the phone and gone out together socially. Kayla confirmed Logan's report of being much calmer and handling frustration better. Logan was able to explain how he had become calmer: self-talk, taking things one at a time so they didn't build up, negotiating with Kayla, relaxing properly after a hard day, being able to quietly tell Kayla what he wants and feeling good about himself.

Interestingly, Logan said that he hadn't been able to do the prediction experiment as he was thinking so hard about what to write on his chart that this affected his behaviour – for the good!

More homework suggestions include the following:

- Continue with what works and pay attention to what else you are doing that is helpful that you hadn't noticed before.

- Do the easiest thing that works.

- Think about what else might help.

- Decide which part of your goal you are going to achieve and do it.

- Where an exception seems to be a coincidence or just luck, try to discover more about it.

(Adapted from Bannink 2010, p.157)

Evaluating the session and ending it

Solution focused practice has no notion of a set length or number of sessions needed to produce change, aiming instead to be minimally involved in a person's life. Each solution focused session is potentially the last session. Where the homework task is to 'do more of it', there is often no need for a second session, although the person may wish to return to report on successes, which are strengthened by telling how they were achieved. Where there is a second or more sessions, there is no need for them to be weekly. When negotiating the homework task, the worker would ask how long it is likely to take the person and that would set the interval between sessions. As we saw earlier in the case of Sophie (see Practice example 6.4), she only needed two sessions, but they were 2 months apart. Minimal intervention is established at the very beginning when the worker asks the person, 'How will you know when you don't need any more help?' It's also important to check that you have covered all that is important to the person, asking questions such as:

- What questions haven't I asked that would have been helpful?

- Are there any questions you would have liked me to ask?

- Are we staying on track with what's important for you to talk about?

- Have I forgotten something important?

Similarly, it is important throughout the process to ask, 'Is what we're talking about interesting to you?'

It is important to evaluate your effectiveness by asking the person how useful the session has been for them. Most people are too polite to say that it's been of no help at all, saying instead that it's been 'a bit useful', so it is helpful to follow up with questions such as:

- Oh, that's not good enough. What would I have been doing if I'd been more helpful?

- If I have a scale of 0–10, where 0 is this session's been of no help at all and 10 is it couldn't have been more helpful, where would you rate this session?

- What would I have been doing differently if you scored the session a point higher?

- Which questions were the most helpful?

- What advice would you give me that I could pass on to someone else with a problem similar to yours?

Feedback

Solution focused practice recognises the importance of constructing helpful feedback for people at the end of sessions in order to build solutions. de Jong and Berg (2002, p.128) identify three main aims of feedback:

- to assist in the development of clear goals

- to focus people on the exceptions that are related to the goals

- to encourage people to notice what they and others may be doing to make the exceptions happen.

Verbal feedback is given at the end of each session as a summary that informs the homework task; however, we find it useful to follow this up with written feedback so that the person has a record of progress – or lack of it – on which to reflect. Written feedback is also important in terms of transparency and accountability; there are serious consequences for people who are violent and they will be concerned about what is written about them. Solution focused work lends itself to being entirely open with the person as there is no hidden agenda behind the questioning of the workers; they are eliciting information from the person and seeking their meanings rather than analysing it from a professional perspective. In this sense it is relatively easy to explain to people how you work, emphasising that they are the person who knows themselves the best, that everyone has the capacity to change and the strength to achieve this, and that your role is to work with them to help discover the solution. This contrasts with some other approaches where the worker is looking for hidden meanings, and it can be difficult to explain the theory behind such interventions.

To assist people in identifying their progress and how they did it, the written feedback is formatted into four sections: problem description, exceptions (what has been done), solutions (how it has been done) and tasks/next steps. Practice example 7.4 shows how feedback is constructed in this way using the person's own words. Feedback notes also constitute an accurate agency record of each session. Some workers find the use of the person's words unprofessional, but to re-author these words would be against the basic assumptions of the approach: honouring the person's knowledge, plus accuracy and transparency.

Practice example 7.5 shows how charts outlining the concerns, goals, safety and progress are used alongside feedback notes where there are formal child protection issues.

PRACTICE EXAMPLE 7.4

Session notes
Name: Kelly

Problem
Kelly has been living on eggshells for almost 3 years. When she married Mark he was kind, considerate, loving – the man she dreamed of, the man whose voice she liked to hear on the phone, the man she liked to lie next to – but he became paranoid, depressed and jealous. When Kelly stood up to his jealous accusations, he became physically violent.

Kelly has left Mark and is getting stronger all the time but needs some answers to questions in her mind. She has love for him still and hopes that he can be helped. She also half believes the things he said to her about his emotional and physical violence being her fault. She would like to talk with him to clear these things up.

She hopes to be well again, then baby Joshua will be fine. She knows she will be all right when little things don't set her back.

Exceptions/progress

- Kelly is being strong by going to live with her mother. She surprised herself by sorting out her money – even though she has fear and panic of being among loads of people. She has been at her sister's house and was all right there. She is eating and sleeping better than she has done in ages, and she is not bursting into tears over little things.

- She is already coping with her feeling of loss. Yesterday was her wedding anniversary and it was not as bad as she thought it would be.

- Kelly is beginning to get back to being herself. Before, Mark had made her feel stupid, ugly and useless. He also partly had her believing that she was the cause of his jealousy, and that he had no control over his violent behaviour.

- All the time that Kelly was living with domestic violence, she still managed to make sure that Joshua was all right and not affected by it.

Thoughts on solutions

- Kelly is being strong for Joshua at the moment – and for herself. She knows she can't let Mark do that to her again. She knows it is time to take care of herself, not Mark.

- She is coping with the feeling of loss partly by being numb, but the main thing is knowing that she loves Mark and cares what happens to him. She also feels relieved that she is safe and that he can't hurt her.

- Kelly knows that she couldn't be the cause of his violent behaviour – he was doing this ages before he met Kelly. (He did a prison sentence for road rage, gets wound up in supermarkets and assaulted her grandfather.) She also knows that he has more control over his behaviour than he admits: when he was hitting her, he managed to pick up the phone, dial his grandmother and talk about his own feelings all at the same time!

- Kelly kept Joshua safe by playing and laughing with him, even when she was really down from the way Mark was treating her.

Homework

- Kelly has decided to write to Mark and tell him she still cares about him and hopes he can sort out his problems. She will enclose a leaflet and referral form for the anger management programme. Then it is up to Mark to take the first step. If he can't be bothered to do something about his behaviour, Kelly will get on with her own life.

- She will do more things for herself, like having her hair cut to shoulder length and, perhaps, dark blonde streaks done. She might wear more of her favourite colour (blue), and she might walk down the road with her head high.

- She will do more of the same for sorting out her life – it is working pretty well so far.

Date and time of next appointment

Kelly will ask for an appointment if she needs one. The covering letter will read as follows:

Dear Kelly,

As promised, here is your copy of the notes. I hope that I have got everything right but, if not, please let me know so that I can make any necessary alterations. I think I may have missed some of the successful things you have done – not many women show such strength, determination and consideration after domestic violence as you have done. This says a lot about you as a person.

All best wishes.

PRACTICE EXAMPLE 7.5

Simon (19 years old), Ricky (14 years old), Kane (13 years old), Beth (12 years old), Chloe (10 years old) and Holly (8 years old) live with foster parents, Bob and Margaret. Simon has severe learning needs and Chloe has moderate learning needs. Table 7.1a provides a safe-care plan for the six children, and Table 7.1b shows the goals of everyone involved.

Table 7.1a Safe-care plan for the six children

Concerns (historic, recent and current)	Evidence of safety	What safety will look like
Simon was found with his trousers round his ankles, holding a family dog astride him (historic).	Social Care found Simon another home, but Margaret rejected it as unsuitable. She is waiting for a place nearer to *her* home.	Simon will be living elsewhere and he will have learned about sexually appropriate behaviour.
Kane and Simon were found with their trousers round their ankles (historic).		Same as above.
Beth disclosed that Kane had dropped his boxer shorts in front of her (recent).	Kane is keeping the rules.	Kane will be fully dressed when out of his bedroom at all times.
Kane went into Chloe's bedroom and sat on her bed. He didn't see that this was inappropriate or what the 'fuss is about' (recent).	Kane accepts that it was pretty serious. He keeps himself apart from Chloe when she gets angry.	Kane will be accepting responsibility for keeping himself safe from allegations and clear about what his safe-care plan looks like.
Ricky and Kane talked inappropriately about sexual matters (e.g. Ricky dared Kane to have sex with Chloe and he would have sex with Beth) (recent).	Ricky has been moved to another placement and a separate safety plan has been drawn up for him.	Kane will have girlfriends outside the home and treat these girls with respect. He will also be more respectful with women generally.

Concerns (historic, recent and current)	Evidence of safety	What safety will look like
Kane is disrespectful to others. He silenced Chloe when she tried to talk about her safety scale (current).	Kane reports that he is being more polite with everyone, especially Bob. He is controlling his moods by going to his bedroom to calm himself down. He reports fewer arguments as he prefers it this way.	Kane will be respectful with the three girls. Especially, he will encourage them to express their own opinions and not talk over them.
Chloe was involved in sexually concerning behaviour with two boys in a taxi when coming home from school (current).	Chloe is working with her key worker on this.	Chloe will have learned about sexually appropriate behaviour.
The three girls are all younger and more biddable than Kane (current).	Chloe is becoming more assertive. The girls keep the rules too.	Margaret has instituted safe-care rules to protect the girls. They are now in one bedroom and the boys are not allowed upstairs, except when changing their school clothes and going to bed.
Margaret is tired of sleeping with 'one ear open' as the children's bedrooms are very close to each other (current).	CCTV has been installed. It isn't as intrusive as Social Care thought – the kids prefer it to the baby alarm that operated previously.	CCTV will have been installed upstairs.

Table 7.1b Goals of everyone involved

Child/young person's goals	Carers' goals	Professionals' goals
Kane just hopes everyone will all shut up and go away, but he is beginning to recognise that he needs to demonstrate safety.	Margaret and Bob would like Kane to have more control over his emotions and be more respectful with other family members.	There will be no further allegations of sexually inappropriate behaviour.

Action plan: As Kane says, people might not believe that he has changed and is safer, so we will look at how to do respectfulness with the whole family at the next session.

Subsequent sessions

When other sessions are necessary, the format of looking for exceptions and progress, exploring possible solutions, summarising, evaluating and negotiating homework is essentially the same as in the first session. It may not be necessary to revisit goals, although people's goals often develop as they make progress. Presuming positive behavioural change, the worker asks, 'What's better?' The more usual conversational openings of 'How are you?' and 'How are things?' are avoided as these encourage problem talk. Asking 'What's better?' shows that we are interested in what has gone well. This is not to say that the difficulties many people experience are ignored; rather, that we are interested in amplifying *any* success, however small. Selekman (1997) suggests that in all subsequent meetings there are four main possibilities: things are either better, the same, worse or mixed.

When things are better

This is the most frequent scenario when working with people who have been violent. Violence usually incurs more costs than benefits, so people are often well motivated to make changes in their lives once they are respected as worthwhile people. When people reply that things are indeed better, it is important not to offer praise; instead, curious questions are asked about what exactly is better, how they did it, where and when they did it and who noticed. In this way, the success is amplified and the person has praised *themselves*. It is important also not to rush into congratulating the person; instead, ask if this progress is enough, or does the person want to do more. People often develop large and ambitious goals once they begin making progress, and it is not our job to lower these goals by expressing satisfaction with small progress. Also, of course, questions that elicit the evidence of safe behaviours are always asked.

PRACTICE EXAMPLE 7.6

This is an extract from the taped recording of the fifth and final session with a boy who at 15 years of age had fallen in love with a 12-year-old boy at school, and was following younger boys to the toilet in supermarkets. Eighteen months later, Adrian is in a new, more supportive peer group. He has fallen in love with a young man in that group. They had a drunken kiss, but then the boy told Adrian he was straight. Adrian is bitterly disappointed (he describes himself as red eyed and mardy) but accepts that the two of them can only have a friendship.

What 'was better' was that he had 'expanded himself'. After talking about how he did this, he was asked some safety questions:

Judith: So, you're a lot happier as well, despite the red eyes and the tears. Overall a lot happier?

Adrian: A lot happier.

Judith: Yes?

Adrian: Yes. Definitely.

Judith: Do you know my scales?

Adrian: Yes.

Judith: Let's do a couple of scales. First of all, the problem at its worst, when 0 is the first time I saw you it was as bad as it got, wasn't it? All right, you had some bad moments as well in the middle, didn't you? And 10 is the problem completely gone. Where are you on that one?

Adrian: Nine...nine and a half.

Judith: Nine and a half. Fascinating. Last time I saw you, you told me you'd settle for eight because you thought there would always be memories and that would be as good as you could get.

Adrian: I'd say the memories are only worth half a point.

Judith: Yes.

Adrian: The memories aren't fresh in your mind. They just... (inaudible).

Judith: And is nine and a half good enough for you?

Adrian: I think so. Yes. I don't think I'd ever get to 10, you know, I may without trying in a few years...(inaudible). I don't...there's definitely no need to make it a 10 because there's not really much difference other than how things...(inaudible). They're just memories.

Judith: So, on young boys being safe from you: if 0 means that they're not at all and 10 means they're completely safe, was it right care?

Adrian: Right love, right care, wrong love, wrong care.

Judith: Right love. If 0 is wrong love, wrong care, where are you on that one?

Adrian: First impressions are I should say is 9 again because these memories I always thought would create a risk because they could become active again. I don't think they will, so I'll say 10, if I'm not being too facetious.

Judith: No.

Adrian: Because I don't ever think they will.

Judith: How do you know that? What are you doing differently that makes you know that for sure?

Adrian: My whole life's different. My whole thinking strategies, coping strategies, things I want, things I don't want. (He talks about changes in his home circumstances which have tested his coping strategies.)

Judith: So you've got a new address now.... What about the happiness scales? (After drawing a scale of 1–100) And this is the pits, despair, and this is blissfully happy. Where are you on that one at the moment?

Adrian: At this precise moment, I'm only probably on 80/85 because I'm overjoyed that I've got things back together with this boy and that he hasn't fallen out with me forever. But saying that, I'm crushed as well because he's not as gay as I wanted him to be and we're back as well to the beginning of that but at the highlight. If you'd asked me that question about 5 seconds afterwards, I'd have shouted 100 at you.

Judith: One hundred and one!

Adrian: Yes, but...

Judith: Suppose we take – it's silly of me to ask this question at your age – but supposing we took sexual relationships out of it, where would you be in terms of where you want your life to be going and happiness?

Adrian: I'd say, I don't know because I feel that I'm not going as far and fast as I want to and as quickly as I wanted to, because I've left education and being pushed by my family back into education in September. But I still don't know whether that's right. I'm used to earning a [more] substantial amount of money than I did, and I'm used to being able to go out with my friends and not having to sit in a classroom all day. That's something I don't want to do. I mean, I want to do something, especially to do with films or drama, and I don't necessarily see how A levels and university will help.

When things are the same

We find that a response of 'nothing's better, absolutely nothing' is more likely from people who have been the victims of violence, partly because, we suspect, people don't expect to recover quickly from serious trauma. Furthermore, the sense of betrayal involved in being hurt by a loved, trusted person goes deep. However, change always happens, so patient questioning about what happened yesterday, what happened the day before, if any part of yesterday is better than another and so forth will yield small exceptions. You could also ask the person how they have managed to prevent things from getting worse, how they have endured all this without losing hope or managing not to go backward. Recognising how they did this leads to the identification of skills and strengths which they can then use to get some forward momentum.

Alternatively, you could say, 'All problems have advantages as well as disadvantages. How can you keep the advantages but still get rid of the problem?' This is a useful question that acknowledges the complexity of problems and their influence on people's lives. For example, problems can seem like 'old friends' in that a label excuses the person from responsibilities they are not yet ready to accept. One woman told us it gave her the excuse not to try anything new, although saying that out loud gave her the determination *to try* something new. You can ask if it suits them to be dominated by the problem. Homework suggestions when progress is slow or the situation is stuck include:

- Each day do one small thing that is good for you. We'll talk about what difference it makes.

- Each day notice what else you can do that's good for you so we can talk about it.

- Keep track of the good choices you make so we can talk about them.

- As you are not yet able to defeat the problem, what can you do to stop it from growing or make it wait? Start with small steps.

- Pretend you have a future and notice the difference so we can talk about it. Notice what you will be doing instead of what you are doing now.

- Do something to be kind to yourself but hard on the problem, then notice what is different.

- Problems try to confuse us, so confuse the problem by taking some control of your thoughts. Think up some things to say to yourself that will help you stand up to the problem and its lies.

- Choose one day and do something really different.

PRACTICE ACTIVITY 7.3

With a colleague, take turns being the worker and the person you are seeing. The worker does nothing but sit and listen attentively and watch non-verbal gestures while the person complains about a personal issue for 5 minutes. The worker then feeds back to the person what qualities have been noticed. These observations must be sincere and pertinent. Examples include: 'I noticed what a persistent person you are', 'You seem to me to be very dedicated to your family', 'How very observant you are' and so forth. The person then tells the worker what the highlight of the exercise was in a couple of sentences. Reverse roles and repeat the exercise.

(Adapted from Lamarre 2005, p.65)

When things are worse

People who report that things are worse often have feelings of hopelessness and helplessness. People's lives can be very difficult due to multiple stresses and long-term problems interacting to make things worse. For example, Tansy's morale was very low after many years of her partner telling her she was so fat and ugly that he could only have sex with her when he didn't have to look at her from the front. He then left her quite suddenly, selling their house behind her back and taking all the furniture with him. She was left on public assistance in a tiny rented house she couldn't really afford, struggling with the impact of years of emotional abuse, grief and loss of her home and partner, as well as poverty. Not surprisingly, her morale was so low that any new issue, however small, set her back. In these instances useful questions can be:

- What has kept your hope alive during all this?

- Suppose you had more hope. How would your life change?

- What is the smallest difference that would give you more hope?

- When did you feel hopeful and how did you manage that? (You may have to go back a long way in a person's life with this question, but it still helps to ask about how that hopeful person saw themselves.)

- If you could consult that hopeful you, what advice would they give you to help with the terrible situation you are in today?

- When you think of hope, what does it look like?

- What does it mean to have survived these traumatic events?

- When have there been times that these terrible things didn't seem quite as bad? What was different then?

- What will you be doing differently when the problems are not affecting your life so much?

- How will you be able to tell when you are handling things a little better or that it's a little easier for you?

With hopelessness, going slowly and gently is the most effective way forward. Take time to focus on questions that help people realise they do have the ability to do at least one small thing each day that is good for them, and develop smaller tasks. For example, Tansy's symbol of hope was a red rose, and her first step toward a future with hope was washing and styling her hair and making an arrangement with artificial roses.

Things being worse due to helplessness are usually associated with the person being powerless to protest about perceived unfairness on the part of powerful people in their lives – parents, teachers, social workers, judges and so forth. The most shocking example of this was when we asked 14-year-old Jonathon's mother to come along to a session after Jonathon told us that all his efforts at controlling his temper were having no effect on family relations. We began by saying that before we start to look at the problem, could we talk first about things that are going right, asking Jonathon's mother to tell us the good things about him, to which she replied in a tone of deadly finality, 'There *aren't* any'.

PRACTICE EXAMPLE 7.7

Rafik's youngest son was made the subject of a care order after Rafik broke his wife's nose while she was holding their baby son. She was living separately from him with their school-age son in the hope of regaining the care of her baby son. The social worker set admirably clear goals for Rafik to be permitted to return home: there would be no arguments between him and his wife, he would set a better example for his older son and this would be evidenced in better relationships with his family. Rafik agreed with these goals and left the first session buoyant about the opportunity to change things.

At his second session he was angry and upset. The social worker had banned him from seeing his wife and older son. She had also told him to solve the family's debt problem by obtaining work. He found work some distance from home but was told he couldn't have contact with his baby son outside office hours. Rafik was in despair.

Rafik was asked how his (justifiable) anger and upset was helping the situation. What sort of response would be most helpful, and what small step could he take to build a better relationship with the social worker? He acknowledged that his anger and upset only 'proved' that he wasn't going to change, so he set himself the goal of being pleasant to the social worker and asking her advice on what his next step should be. Particularly, he would ask her how best he could maintain contact with his baby son when he was working long hours some distance away.

Often things are worse because the person has forgotten to do something that had been working before. Eleven-year-old Sally had been fighting with her brother much less and undertaking household chores without being verbally abusive but came to her third session with her mother on the verge of tears. They had had a monumental argument. Their upset was acknowledged, but rather than focusing on what had gone wrong, they were asked what progress Sally had made with her goals, which was substantial. The mother was asked if there was anything she had forgotten to do that had worked previously and, yes, she had been tired and forgot to do *her* self-calming as they were outside and she was worried the neighbours would hear. (For more details, see Milner and O'Byrne 2002, pp.89–90.)

When things are mixed

By this time, you will be getting the hang of the sort of questions that maintain progress, so rather than give any examples, we end this chapter with the challenge below.

PRACTICE ACTIVITY 7.4

Think of a person with whom you are working who always seems to take a step or two back after going forward. This can be very frustrating and have the effect of getting you to offer advice and do all the work. Take a few minutes to reflect on how you have been responding, and then formulate questions that will get the person thinking constructively.

Chapter 8

Groupwork

Using connections

Solution focused groupwork is in some ways a contradiction in terms. If we hold firmly to the view that each person is unique and we eschew labelling, why would we then story them as sufficiently similar to others in a group? Neither does groupwork fit with the solution focused aim of minimal intervention in people's lives as group members are expected to complete a set number of sessions on a topic they have not chosen:

> In groupwork, if the members were each to choose unrelated outcomes, there is a danger they would become a collection of individuals who happen to be sitting in the same room, taking turns to talk, rather than members of a group who are connected and can, thereby, have more of an impact on each other. (Shennan 2014, p.170)

Despite these limitations, groupwork has proved effective in working with people who are violent (see, for example, Young, undated; Lee *et al.* 2003; Shin 2009) and people who have experienced violence (see, for example, Levy-Peck 2014).

Advantages of groupwork

Groupwork has the advantage of utilising the group processes of support, learning, optimism and the opportunity to help others. Group support comes from the person realising that they are not alone, that others experience the same feelings which, in the context of violence, are often to do with shame, embarrassment and fear of humiliation. We invited a small group of mothers whose children's behaviour was sexually harmful to help workers redesign the service's guidebook for parents. One parent's account of her reaction to finding out about her son's behaviour – 'I thought, I'll have to move' – triggered a wave of relief as the other mothers shared their reactions (Milner 2006). Group members benefit also from listening to others' solutions, questioning these solutions and adapting them to their own situations. They can report back on their successes and receive encouragement.

PRACTICE EXAMPLE 8.1

Members of a safety group for teenage girls at risk of sexual exploitation by older men were discussing whether the use of a condom would spoil a man's enjoyment of sex. The conversation went round in circles until Kylie said, 'I'll ask my boyfriend'. She rang him with the phone on loudspeaker, so everyone heard his reply – 'How should I know? I've never [expletive] used one' – at which point she politely thanked him for the information and ended the call. After the gales of laughter died down, they talked about his lack of respect for Kylie. At the next session Kylie reported that she had dumped her boyfriend and Rochelle had dumped her boyfriend too: 'I asked him if he'd use a Johnny (condom) and he said no, so I told him where he could go. Good riddance, I've got a new boyfriend now and he's respectful'. (Milner 2003, pp.50–56)

Sharry (2007) maintains that solution focused groups can be fun, enjoyable and energetic experiences for members. Not only do members learn from the experiences of other group members, but this also gives them hope and optimism that their solutions are feasible. Also, the opportunity to help others gives members a chance to be of value and learn to *be* valued.

Setting up a group

Time spent on planning is essential, particularly being clear regarding what you have to offer, when you can start and how many sessions you are offering. We learned the hard way on this: when asked to establish a groupwork programme for adults who are violent, we carefully prepared a leaflet explaining the programme, distributing it to all agencies in contact with both offenders and victims of domestic violence (Milner and Jessop 2003). Fortunately, we offered a pre-group assessment appointment as our first referrals consisted of three white, heterosexual men, two of whom failed to attend, while the third did not want to wait for the group to start. Lee *et al.* (2003) find it not unusual for people to become highly motivated to seek help as a court date looms, but they do not find that this affects outcomes. Our next two referrals were white, lesbian women, so we began individual work and our group never got off the ground. Consulting with potential referrers is an important component of the planning stage, especially those referring young people whom you suspect may see your group as a convenient repository for their 'problem' kids.

You also need to decide on the number of sessions, how long they will last and the spacing of them. The solution focused answer to these issues is to be as time limited as possible; members who want the group to continue after the course ends may well form their own self-help group, as did our parents of children whose children had offended sexually (Milner 2006). Different groups require different lengths of time per session. Where people are able to talk freely, short sessions are ideal, but you may need to allow longer for people who are not used to talking about their behaviour. We find that men who have been violent to their partners take time to begin expressing themselves, especially where they have been used to answering difficulties with their fists. Teenagers usually talk very freely but need time to settle down; and people with learning difficulties will lose concentration if the sessions are too long. As change happens between sessions and people need time to try out new behaviours, solution focused groups often hold the first two or three groups at weekly intervals and increase the amount of time between later sessions (Selekman 1993; Lee *et al.* 2003); however, O'Connell (2001) makes the point that some programmes may be better held as 1- or 2-day courses.

It is also important to provide a safe environment for your groupwork. There are obvious 'givens' here such as confidentiality assurances, turn taking and non-blaming talk. You will also need to decide whether you can run the group on your own or have a co-facilitator. Lee *et al.* (2003) use a female and male facilitator, finding it helpful to have one person looking on and interposing questions where they see the need for another viewpoint. Asking a person to leave the group also needs thinking through carefully, the process being made clear in group rules. Furthermore, do not forget the physical environment; sitting in a circle is not the only way to encourage people to communicate.

You may need room to paint or do drama. You may need transport or facilities for drying off dripping clothes if your group members use public transport. Are you going to provide refreshments? With our mothers' group mentioned earlier, we provided transport, child care facilities and food, flip charts, paper, crayons and more. The mothers were surprised and delighted that we had gone to so much trouble and it helped them get down to work quickly. As we commented earlier, treating the person as worthwhile is an important practice principle of solution focused work, and it pays dividends. The mothers not only started a support group for parents using the service but also became confident enough to address an international conference (Milner 2006).

PRACTICE ACTIVITY 8.1

Identify a small group of people with whom you are working and decide what sort of group is most appropriate for these people. Will it be a single session, topic-centred or self-help group? Draft a publicity leaflet for your group.

Determining group rules

If you are working with an individual and they are late for an appointment, the consequence is simply that they have less time that session. As you set later appointments according to the time the person thinks it will take them to undertake agreed tasks, there is no need to worry unduly about attendance. With a group, attendance is more salient. Do you sit with a group of people waiting for a latecomer to arrive, or do you begin on time and then face the problem of how the latecomer can catch up? In groupwork, rules are important. Lee *et al.* (2003) explain them matter-of-factly, with respect, and without confrontation or argument. Their first rule is on attendance: members are expected to be punctual, and if they miss more than one session, they will be terminated from the programme (although they may repeat the programme later). This sounds harsh, but they explain that a time commitment is necessary as the groupwork is important and has value for the participants' lives, and that they do not want members to miss anything that will be of value. Their group members are referred by the court as an alternative to a custodial sentence but, even so, if your group is anything other than a drop-in group, this is a sensible rule.

Other important rules Lee *et al.* (2003) impose are to do with participation in the group and goal setting. Members are expected to discuss and share their ideas, and treat disagreements with respect. The authors explain that their input is valued. Shyness is dealt with by stressing that they often note that a shy person may offer important perspectives that would otherwise go unnoticed. This opens up opportunities for people to talk about their own shyness. Because solution focused groupwork is essentially individual work in a group setting (Banks 2005), a further rule they set is that everyone must have a goal by the end of the third session. This is to ensure that each person has an outcome and cannot simply claim that attending the group is sufficient effort on their part:

> The goal must be something you choose to do differently that improves your life and something that other people can notice and be affected by. If you don't have a goal by the third session, you will not be able to continue. (Lee *et al.* 2003, p.45)

Other rules relate to safety issues: any sort of violence will not be tolerated, everything discussed in the group stays in the group, there will be no blaming talk and attending the group under the influence of alcohol or drugs will lead the person to being discharged from the group. These rules are set by the group facilitator, but other rules can be decided by the group. For example, some people can be disruptive to a group, so it may be necessary to agree on any other behaviours that would lead to dismissal from the group.

PRACTICE EXAMPLE 8.2

A group for young Indigenous men in Australia used a 'bench system' for rule breaches on the grounds that the boys play football, relate to it and respect it:

> Each week one student is the designated umpire. If one of the kids breaks one of the ground rules (which have been established by the group) then the umpire gives a warning. For a second break the student is sent off – 'sin binned' for a length of time decided by the group. When they come back, they are expected to apologize and talk about what happened calmly. A third break involves a meeting with the principal and possible expulsion from the group. But this rarely happens.

(Couzens 1999, pp.24–25)

Groups working with people who have chaotic lives or are situated in institutions, such as prisons and hospitals, where the populations change over at short notice, will need fewer rules and more consultation with group members on what they hope to achieve.

Groupwork practice principles

Solution focused groups follow the practice principles outlined in previous chapters, although creativity is required to make them relevant to the group setting. All groupwork begins with goal setting. People who have been violent are likely to be anxious and poorly focused, so it is important to help them form a goal by clarifying vague goals, simplifying complex goals and moving a big goal to a smaller, doable one through curious questioning. Sharry (2007) suggests that using problem-free talk as an icebreaker can reassure people that they are valued as people and not defined by their problem. He asks each person to say their name and reveal a secret talent they have or a hobby they would like to take up. Although group members helping each other is an advantage of groupwork, in the early, goal-forming stage, this is not particularly helpful, so you might want to acknowledge it but focus the person back on working on the goal by saying something like, 'So that's a few ideas for you; do any of them fit, or have you a better idea of your own?'

Sharry suggests a simple process to establish goals that can be used or varied depending on the facilitator and group:

1. Members can be invited to complete a goal questionnaire (see Figure 8.1).

2. They are then invited to work in pairs to share their goals and to discuss what they would like to get out of coming to the group.

3. Members are then invited to complete a 'group round' – each member speaks in turn, stating their goal for coming to the group. The facilitator has an important role during this round, in helping members frame positive goals, in making links between common goals and drawing in other members appropriately.

4. The facilitator (or a nominated person) records the goals on a flip chart which is put on public display and kept as a reference for subsequent sessions.

(Sharry 2007, p.110)

Initial Goal Form

Name: Date:

We are committed to helping you get the most out this group. Filling in this questionnaire will help you to be really clear about your goals and thus help us work together to adapt the course to best suit everyone.

By coming to this group, what are your goals? What would you like to achieve?

Please rate between 1 and 10 how close you are to these goals (where 1 means the furthest away you have been and 10 is when you will have achieved your goal completely).

Goal 1	Goal 2
Far away Achieved	Far away Achieved
1 2 3 4 5 6 7 8 9 10	1 2 3 4 5 6 7 8 9 10

What steps have you already taken towards your goals?

What strengths, skills and resources do you bring to the course to ensure you will achieve these goals?

Figure 8.1 Initial Goal Form. (Sharry 2007, p.111)

Shennan (2014) uses the idea of developing a group theme (Pichot 2009) by having one word representing each member's desired outcome by asking what difference it will make. One word answers, such as calm, patient or happy, will need clarifying, but at this stage they provide a connection between members.

The do's and don'ts of groupwork are as follows:

• Do persist in the pursuit of a clear, well-formed goal.

- Do pursue the details.

- Don't get sidetracked by other issues.

- Don't suggest a goal or work harder than the participant.

- Do restate a goal when it is well defined.

- Do use a scaling question to help participants state their commitment to the goal.

- Do notice efforts to cooperate.

- Do ignore non-goal-related comments and redirect attention to the pursuit of goals.

(Adapted from Lee *et al.* 2003, p.72)

As with individual work, goals can be established through any of the techniques of scaling questions, the miracle question, best hopes and so forth, the advantage of the group setting being that you can use them creatively. (For a fuller description, see Sharry 2007.) Another advantage of a groupwork setting is the use of space. You can set out a scale on the floor and ask members to stand on the number that represents their progress toward their goal. Then they can be interviewed by another group member on how they got to that number and what their next steps are.

PRACTICE EXAMPLE 8.3

In the teenage girls' group mentioned earlier (see Practice example 8.1), goals were set by inviting them to interview each other using a set of strengths cards[1] and list their findings on a flip chart. They also listed the strengths they didn't have but would like to have. Despite their earlier boasting about wild, exciting lifestyles with older men, they all wanted to be happy and cheerful. A 1–100 happiness scale was drawn on the flip chart and they were invited to locate their current state of happiness.

Writing on the flip chart was much enjoyed and the conversation became cooperative as they shared experiences of brief moments of happiness and wrote them for all to see. Insults about spelling changed into helpfulness 'that's not how you f*****g spell happiness, you silly cow'; 'well, you f*****g know I missed three f*****g years

---

1   Website: www.stlukes.org.uk

at high school, 'course I can't spell'; "ere Marie, you're a right good f*****g speller, tell Kylie how to f*****g spell happiness'. Enjoyment of flip chart recording and a determination to ensure that words were neatly written and correctly spelled remained a feature of subsequent groups.

(Adapted from Milner 2003)

Sharry (2007, pp.124–125) outlines a Session Plan for an Out-Patient 'Anger Management and Handling Conflict' Group (see Practice example 8.4). This is an integrated solution focused group which combines psycho-educational input on communication skills and conflict resolution with a solution focused group process. It illustrates the process involved in planning a programme and provides a framework for working with a group of people who are there because of their violence.

PRACTICE EXAMPLE 8.4

Session 1

- Introductory 'getting to know one another' exercises and icebreakers.

- Goal setting and ground-rule negotiation.

- Explanation of topic – discussion on the purpose of anger and the effect of conflict in clients' lives. Facilitator introduces some reframes about the positive functions of anger and the opportunities involved in conflict resolution.

- Planning – during the following week, clients are encouraged to notice the time they get angry or are involved in conflict, particularly noticing the exceptions, the times they feel positively in control or able to manage conflict well.

Sessions 2–8
The middle sessions follow roughly the same structure as follows:

- Introduction.

- Review of week – facilitated discussion of how each client got on during the previous week, attending in particular to exceptions to the problem, or times when they were closer to their goals for the group.

- New topic – a new skills topic is introduced over the 7 weeks as follows:

- Making a connection/building rapport.
- Active listening.
- Speaking up assertively.
- Remaining calm 1 (using relaxation and breathing techniques).
- Remaining calm 2 (using positive self-talk).
- Problem solving – finding good solutions.
- Bringing it all together – using all skills learned in real examples.

- Skills practice – in small groups the clients practise the introduced ideas using exercises and role-play with examples from their own lives.
- Homework/planning – suggested 'homework' is given and in small groups clients plan how they will apply this in their own situation.
- Conclusion and recap.

Session 9 (final session)

- Review of course material.
- Review of course goals.
- Planning for what next. What further support is needed to keep on track?
- Award ceremony – to mark achievements thus far.
- Group feedback – each member is given the opportunity to provide feedback to the group and other individuals.
- Close.

Managing difficult group members

It's rare that an entire group is difficult, and when they are it's usually down to poor planning, especially not consulting adequately with referrers. Again we found this out the hard way: after our success with the young women's group, where the young women developed the referrer's complex goal of safety into detailed goals of gaining self-respect, better relationships with mothers, proper boyfriends and a job over the course of the group, we failed miserably with a young men's group referred by the same pupil referral unit. The teachers were hoping for the same positive outcomes from the young men, but we found goal setting to be impossible. The young men had been told by teachers that this group was a private place where they could talk about anything they wanted; nothing they said would be reported back to staff. This was an invitation too far for a group of hormonally charged youngsters; talking about what they wanted turned out mostly to be pornography, much of it on their mobile phones. This excited them and made it impossible to start any useful discussion about goals. Neither was it possible to agree on group rules after the group members had been given carte blanche by their teachers. More time talking about preferred outcomes and boundaries with the referrers would have prevented the debacle we presided over for two sessions before abandoning the groupwork. We expect groups for adolescents to be rowdy and allow some settling time; providing refreshments helps as does a version of musical chairs: we set out chairs for a scaling question but number some seats more than once and leave some numbers out. This allows members to race for the 'right' chair, complain about the 'mistakes' in numbering and then we put them in charge of sorting it all out and redoing the exercise.

Usually difficulties arise in groups when one or two members talk too much or too little. It is relatively easy to encourage quiet group members to talk. As we mentioned earlier, you can set 'contributing' as a group rule and introduce a discussion about shyness. Alternatively, you can start off by saying that you are about to ask each member a question in turn. This means that shy people have to say something and you are establishing turn taking. For people who talk too much, you can remind the group that respectfulness means a speaking member is listened to without interruption; or you could wait until the talkative member draws breath and ask the rest of the group, 'Of all the suggestions X has made, can you choose one that might be useful to you?'

When a group member is unduly negative about the group, you can remain curious: 'What will the group be doing differently when you are finding it useful?' and, importantly, 'What will you be doing differently when the group is more useful to *you*?' And, of course, you can ask all the questions listed in previous chapters. Evaluating how the group is working for members – how, when, where – also helps members become more cooperative, as does carefully crafted recording.

The teenage girls' group discussed earlier (see Practice example 8.1) valued written comments on their contributions to the group; especially as 'naughty girls' in a pupil referral unit, they rarely heard good things about themselves. Good things – strengths, resources, talents, personal qualities – are always worth noticing. We're not suggesting lavish praise, just quiet acknowledgement.

Flexible groupwork in testing situations

It is not always possible to identify a 'target' population in need of groupwork, plan the programme systematically and work with referrers. There are many times when a more flexible approach is needed. For example, Swedish social worker Britta Severin (2001) was asked to run a group for sexual offenders serving long prison sentences, most of whom were not native Swedish speakers. Imaginatively, she interviewed a group of four prisoners separately with the other three prisoners and prison staff looking on. The prison staff spontaneously began to encourage the inmates to pursue their ideas between sessions. Obviously a short, time-limited groupwork programme is not suitable for this population, but the development of small, doable goals *is* suitable.

Similarly, psychiatric day-hospital populations require a flexible approach. Hawkes *et al.* (1998) ran an open group with members joining when they wanted and choosing their own frequency of attendance. The only limit was no more than 15 people per group. Groups took on a workshop feel with members being taught solution focused techniques and interviewing each other. Whole sessions devoted to exploring the miracle question were not unusual, and wall charts, paper and pens for writing down group ideas and displaying them proved useful.

PRACTICE ACTIVITY 8.2

Consider the application of these ideas to the people with whom you work.

- How would you go about teaching them the techniques of solution focused interviewing?
- What media would you use?

Groups sometimes develop a life of their own. As we saw earlier with our parents' group, not only was a support group established for new parents of children with sexually harmful behaviour referred to the service, but also the original group broadcast their success at an international conference. This was no small feat as these women had not even travelled outside their hometown alone before. They were so pleased with their newfound confidence that they celebrated on arrival at conference town by waiting in the queue to travel in a bright pink taxi. Successful groupworkers know when to hand over the group to members and allow them to develop their own ideas.

PRACTICE EXAMPLE 8.4

Teachers at Selwyn College, Auckland, New Zealand, set up an anti-harassment team of students to work with troubled students on the grounds that students were more likely to talk to other students more freely than with adults. The team was successful in dealing with the victims of bullying and harassment, but they felt powerless to change situations. They came up with the idea of mediation, so the school supplied them with training in mediation skills. The turning point in students realising that mediations can change situations came when a group of girls living in a street with a tough reputation held a 'street mediation' along the lines of what they had experienced at school. They reported that they had 'sorted heaps of things out' with 'everyone saying their bit'. Students became so familiar with mediation that they would come up to the team at break times and request a mediation.

The level of skill developed by student members of the team is amazing:

Sometimes it's hard to stay even handed but it's really important so the people feel it's a place where they can speak their mind... If I keep on asking whoever called the mediation, who is most likely to be the victim, 'How did that feel to you?' and then I find myself asking the other person 'Why did you do that?' then I know I'm off track. That's an extreme example! If I find myself doing that though, I quickly start to ask the same questions to each person. I have to stay very aware. Usually when I ask the questions I keep it pretty monotone, that way everyone feels as if they've been treated equally and they've had an equal chance of saying what they need to say. (Lewis and Cheshire 1999, p.114)

Forgotten victims

Many older people in violent relationships have been so ground down by their long-lasting experiences that the violence remains hidden. Working in palliative care Wright (2003) discovered that knowledge that their own, or their partner's, death was imminent – knowing that the violence they had suffered in silence for years was about to end – enabled women to start to break the silence around the abuse they had suffered. For example:

> Kath, aged 79 years and married 58 years, and the carer of Ron, said, 'My marriage has been terrible, terrible, a lifetime of it'. After Ron's death, Kath said, 'I feel a great relief and peace now'.

> Gladys, aged 67 years, married to Bert for 47 years, who really had only a brief time to tell some of her story before she died, said, 'Dying will be a release from him for me. It is a comfort to know that I haven't done anything wrong, that it wasn't my fault'.

The women told their stories only after being asked about how life had been for them. They all said that it made a difference for them that they were given a chance, however small, to tell in safety what life had been like for them, and that they were relieved.

This account reminds us that partner violence becomes even more complicated in the later stages of life where a person ends up being the carer of, or cared for by, a partner who has made their life a misery; for example, Hanson and Maroney (1999, p.105) cite an HIV-positive man whose abusive partner taunted him: 'Who's going to want a sick old fairy like you?' This has implications for how we run reminiscence groups, ensuring we remember to ask questions which allow for violence stories to emerge rather than being repressed within the 'culture of niceness' that surrounds much palliative care.

PRACTICE ACTIVITY 8.3

Thinking about the people with whom you work, are there people whose experiences of violence have been silenced by circumstances? Would they benefit from groupwork? How would you go about planning this groupwork?

References

Alcoholics Anonymous (1976) *Alcoholics Anonymous: The Story of How Thousands of Men and Women Have Recovered from Alcoholism* (aka 'The Big Book'). New York, NY: Alcoholics Anonymous World Services.

Anderson, K.M. (2013) 'Assessing Strengths: Identifying Acts of Resistance to Violence and Oppression.' In D. Saleebey (ed.) *The Strengths Perspective in Social Work Practice* (6th ed.). London: Pearson.

Banks, R. (2005) 'Solution-focused group therapy.' *Journal of Family Psychotherapy 16*, 17–21.

Bannink, F. (2006) *1001 Solution-focused Questions.* London: W.W. Norton.

Bannink, F. (2010) *Handbook of Solution-focused Conflict Management.* Göttingen: Hogrefe Publishing.

Bateman, J. and Milner, J. (2015) *Children and Young People Whose Behaviour is Sexually Concerning or Harmful: Assessing Risk and Developing Safety Plans.* London: Jessica Kingsley Publishers.

Benard, B. and Truebridge, S. (2013) 'A Shift in Thinking: Influencing Social Workers' Beliefs About Individual and Family Resilience in an Effort to Enhance Well-being and Success for All.' In D. Saleebey (ed.) *The Strengths Perspective in Social Work Practice* (6th ed.). London: Pearson.

Berg, I.K. (1994) *Family Based Services: A Solution-focused Approach.* New York, NY: W.W. Norton.

Berg, I.K. and Miller, S. (1992) *Working with the Problem Drinker: A Solution-focused Approach.* New York, NY: W.W. Norton.

Berg, I.K. and Reuss, N.H. (1998) *Solutions. Step by Step. A Substance Abuse Treatment Manual.* London: W.W. Norton.

Burr, V. (2003) *An Introduction to Social Constructionism* (2nd ed.). London: Routledge.

Carpenter, J. (2012) 'Anthony Worral Thompson: I'm just overwhelmed by all this support.' *Daily Express*, 11 January, 2012.

Clark, M.D. (2013) 'The Strengths Perspective in Criminal Justice.' In D. Saleeby (ed.) *The Strengths Perspective in Social Work Practice* (6th ed.). London: Pearson.

Couzens, A. (1999) 'Sharing the Load: Group Conversations with Young Indigenous Men.' In *Extending Narrative Therapy: A Collection of Practice-Based Papers.* Adelaide: Dulwich Centre Publications.

de Jong, P. and Berg, I.K. (2002) *Interviewing for Solutions* (2nd ed.). Pacific Grove, CA: Brooks/Cole.

de Shazer, S. (1988) *Clues: Investigating Solutions in Brief Therapy.* New York, NY: W.W. Norton.

de Shazer, S. (1991) *Putting Difference to Work.* London: W.W. Norton.

Denborough, D. (1996) *Beyond Prison: Gathering Dreams of Freedom*. Adelaide: Dulwich Centre Publications.

Derrida, J. (1973) *Writing and Difference*. Chicago, IL: Chicago University Press.

Dolan, Y. (1998) *One Small Step: Moving from Trauma to a Life of Joy*. Watsonville, CA: Papier-Mache Press.

Durrant, M. (1993) *Creative Strategies for School Problems*. Epping, NSW, Australia: Eastwood Centre.

Essex, S., Gumbleton, J. and Luger, C. (1996) 'Resolutions: Working with families where responsibility is denied.' *Child Abuse Review 5*, 191–201.

Freeman, J., Epston, D. and Lobovits, D. (1997) *Playful Approaches to Serious Problems*. London: W.W. Norton.

Gondolf, E.W. and White, R.J. (2001) 'Batterer program participants who repeatedly assault: Psychopathic tendencies and other disorders.' *Journal of Interpersonal Violence 16*, 361–380.

Hackett, P. (2005) 'Ever Appreciating Circles.' In T.S. Nelson (ed.) *Education and Training in Solution-focused Brief Therapy*. New York, NY: The Haworth Press.

Hampton, B. (1993) *Prisons and Women*. Sydney: University of New South Wales Press.

Hanson, B. and Maroney, T. (1999) 'HIV and Same-Sex Violence.' In B. Leventhal and S.E. Lundy (eds) *Same-Sex Violence: Strategies for Change*. London: Sage.

Hawkes, D., Marsh, T.I. and Wilgosh, R. (1998) *Solution-focused Therapy. A Handbook for Professionals*. Oxford: Butterworth Heinemann.

Jenkins, A. (1990) *Invitations to Responsibility: The Therapeutic Engagement of Men Who Are Violent and Abusive*. Adelaide: Dulwich Centre Publications.

Jenkins, A. (1996) 'Moving Towards Respect: A Quest for Balance.' In C. McClean, M. Carey and M. Whites (eds) *Men's Ways of Being*. Oxford: Westview Press.

Jenkins, A. (2005a) 'Making It Fair: Respectful and Just Intervention with Disadvantaged Young People Who Have Abused.' In M. Calder (ed.) *Children and Young People Who Sexually Abuse: New Theory Research and Practice Developments*. Lyme Regis: Russell House.

Jenkins, A. (2005b) 'Knocking on Shame's Door: Facing Shame Without Shaming Disadvantaged Young People Who Have Abused.' In M. Calder (ed.) *Children and Young People Who Sexually Abuse. New Theory Research and Practice Developments*. Lyme Regis: Russell House.

Lamarre, J. (2005) 'Complaining Exercise.' In T. Nelson (ed.) *Education and Training in Solution-focused Brief Therapy*. London: The Haworth Press.

Lee, M.Y., Sebold, J. and Uken, A. (2003) *Solution-focused Treatment of Domestic Violence Offenders: Accountability for Change*. Oxford: Oxford University Press.

Levy-Peck, J.Y. (2014) 'Forming and Facilitating Support Groups for Survivors of Intimate Partner Sexual Violence.' In L. Ormond-Plummer, P. Easteal and J.Y. Levy-Peck (eds) *Intimate Partner Sexual Violence: A Multidisciplinary Guide to Improving Services and Support for Survivors of Rape and Abuse*. London: Jessica Kingsley Publishers.

Lewis, D. and Cheshire, A. (1999) 'Taking the Hassle Out of School: The Work of the Anti-harassment Team.' In *Extending Narrative Therapy: A Collection of Practice-Based Papers*. Australia: Dulwich Centre Publications.

Lipchik, E. (2000) *Beyond Technique in Solution-focused Therapy: Working with Emotions and the Therapeutic Relationship*. New York, NY: Guilford Press.

Lipchik, E. and Kubicki, A.D. (1996) 'Solution-focused Domestic Violence: Bridges Towards a New Reality in Couples Therapy.' In S.D. Miller and B.L. Duncan (eds) *Handbook of Solution-focused Therapy*. San Francisco, CA: Jossey-Bass.

Lipchik, E. and Turnell, A. (1999) 'The role of empathy in brief therapy: The overlooked but vital context.' *The Australian and New Zealand Journal of Family Therapy 20*, 29–36.

Luthar, S.S., Cicchetti, D. and Becker, B. (2000) 'The construct of resilience: A critical evaluation and guidelines for future research.' *Child Development 71*, 543–562.

Miller, G. (1997) *Becoming Miracle Workers: Language and Meaning in Brief Therapy.* New Brunswick, NJ: Transaction Publishers.

Miller, W.R. and Rollnick, S. (2002) *Motivational Interviewing: Preparing People to Change Addictive Behaviour.* New York, NY: Guilford Press.

Milner, J. (2001) *Women and Social Work: Narrative Approaches.* Basingstoke: Palgrave.

Milner, J. (2003) 'Narrative groupwork with young women – and their mobile phones.' *International Journal of Narrative Therapy and Community Work 3*, 54–60.

Milner, J. (2004a) 'From "disappearing" to "demonized": The effects on men and women of professional interventions based on challenging men who are violent.' *Critical Social Policy 24*, 79–101.

Milner, J. (2004b) 'Groupwork with young women.' *Context 74*, 14–17.

Milner, J. (2006) 'From stigma and isolation to strength and solidarity: parents talking about their experiences of caring for children whose behaviour has been sexually concerning or harmful.' *International Journal of Narrative Therapy and Community Work 2*, 53–60.

Milner, J. (2008) 'Working with people who are violent to their partners: A safety building approach.' *Liverpool Law Review 29*, 67–80.

Milner, J. and Bateman, J. (2011) *Working with Children and Teenagers Using Solution-focused Approaches.* London: Jessica Kingsley Publishers.

Milner, J. and Jessop, D. (2003) 'Domestic violence: Narratives and solutions.' *Probation Journal 50*, 2, 127–148.

Milner, J. and O'Byrne, P. (2002) *Assessment in Social Work* (2nd ed.). Basingstoke: Palgrave.

Milner, J. and Myers, S. (2007) *Working with Violence: Policies and Practices in Risk Assessment and Management.* Palgrave Macmillan: London.

Milner, J. and Singleton, T. (2008) 'Domestic violence: Solution-focused practice with men and women who are violent.' *Journal of Family Therapy 30*, 1, 29–53.

Milner, J., Myers, S. and O'Byrne, P. (2015) *Assessment in Social Work* (4th ed.). Basingstoke: Palgrave.

Murray Parkes, C. (1972) *Bereavement: Studies of Grief in Adult Life.* London: Penguin.

Myers, S. (2007) *Solution-focused Approaches.* Lyme Regis: Russell House.

Myers, S. (2008) *Solution-focused Approaches.* Russell House Publishing: Dorset.

Myers, S. and Milner, J. (2007) *Sexual Issues in Social Work.* Bristol: The Polity Press.

O'Connell, B. (2001) *Solution-focused Stress Counselling.* London: Continuum.

O'Hanlon, B. (1995) 'Breaking the Bad Trance.' Presentation, BRIEF Annual Conference, London, July.

Pichot, T. (with Smock, S.) (2009) *Solution-focused Substance Abuse Treatment.* New York, NY: Routledge.

Reivich, K. and Shatte, A. (2003) *The Resilience Factor: 7 Keys to Finding Your Inner Strength and Overcoming Life's Hurdles.* London: Broadway Books.

Royal College of Psychiatrists (1996) *Assessment and Clinical Management of Risk of Harm to Other People, Council Report CR53.* London: Royal College of Psychiatrists.

Saleebey, D. (2013) 'The Strengths Approach to Practice Beginnings.' In D. Saleebey (ed.) *The Strengths Perspective in Social Work* (6th ed.). London: Pearson.

Selekman, M. (1993) *Pathways to Change: Brief Therapy Solutions to Difficult Adolescents.* New York: Guildford Press.

Selekman, M.D. (1997) *Solution-focused Therapy with Children.* London: Guildford Press.

Selekman, M.D. (2002) *Living on the Razor's Edge.* London: W.W. Norton.

Selekman, M.D. (2007) *The Optimistic Child. A Proven Program to Safeguard Children Against Depression and Build Lifelong Resilience.* New York, NY: Houghton Mifflin.

Severin, B. (2001) 'A Group for Sexual Offenders in Prison.' Presentation, European Brief Therapy Association Conference, Dublin.

Sharry, J. (2001) *Solution-focused Groupwork.* London: Sage.

Sharry, J. (2007) *Solution-focused Groupwork* (2nd ed.). London: Sage.

Sharry, J., Madden, B. and Darmody, M. (2012) *Becoming a Solution Detective: A Strengths-Based Guide to Brief Therapy: Second Edition.* New York: Routledge.

Shennan, G. (2014) *Solution-focused Practice: Effective Communication to Facilitate Change.* Basingstoke: Palgrave Macmillan.

Shin, S.-K. (2009) 'Effects of a Solution-focused Program on the reduction of aggressiveness and the improvement of social readjustment for Korean youth probationers.' *Journal of Social Science Research 35*, 274–284.

Teft, P. (1999) 'Work with men who are violent to their partners: Time to re-assert a pro-feminist analysis.' *Probation Journal 46*, 11–18.

Turnell, A. and Edwards, S. (1999) *Signs of Safety: A Solution and Safety Orientated Approach to Child Protection Casework.* New York, NY: W.W. Norton.

Turnell, A. and Essex, S. (2006) *Working with 'Denied' Child Abuse: The Resolutions Approach.* Maidenhead: Open University Press.

Watling, T. (2012) *Mediation Skills and Strategies: A Practical Guide.* London: Jessica Kingsley Publishers.

Wheeler, J. (2005) 'Solution-focused Training for Social Workers'. In T.S. Nelson (ed.) *Education and Training in Solution-focused Brief Therapy.* New York, NY: The Haworth Press.

White, M. (1995) *Re-authoring Lives: Interviews and Essays.* Adelaide: Dulwich Centre Publications.

White, M. and Epston, D. (1990) *Narrative Means to Therapeutic Ends.* New York, NY: W.W. Norton.

Wittgenstein, L. (1980) *Remarks on the Philosophy of Psychology.* Oxford: Blackwell.

Wright, J. (2003) 'Considering issues of domestic violence and abuse in palliative care and bereavement situations.' *International Journal of Narrative Therapy and Community Work 3*: 72–77.

Young, S. (undated) *Solution-focused Schools. Antibullying and Beyond.* London: BT Press.

Index

accountability 19–20
Alcoholics Anonymous 85
Anderson, K.M. 24
assessment
  evaluating the session 130–6
  of likelihood of change 110–2
  of progress 112–20
  safety assessment process 57–62
assumptions, of solutions focused
    approaches 21–4

Banks, R. 148
Bannink, F. 52, 80, 81, 82, 98, 124, 130
Bateman, J. 14, 28, 37, 54, 66,
    84, 92, 99, 110, 123
Becker, B. 25
Benard, B. 24
Berg, I.K. 18, 21, 47, 73, 93, 126, 132
Burr, V. 15

carers 157
challenging the person 20, 27, 32
Cheshire, A. 156
children, involving 77–8, 109
Cicchetti, D. 25
circular shortened miracle question 77–8
Clark, M.D. 15, 36, 94
coin-tossing task 128
compliance 94
conflicting goals 80–4
confronting the person 20, 27, 32
constructive conversations
  don'ts for 41–2
  do's for 39–41
  group strengths 94–5
  questions 34–6
  socially isolated people 96–8

starting the conversation 88–92
strengths-searching questions 98–101
survival questions 92–4
constructive safety goals 65–8
continuum (safety-danger) 103
conversations see constructive
    conversations; externalising
    conversations
cooperative partnership 34–5
coping questions 92–4
Couzens, A. 30, 148
creative thinking 121–3

Darmody, M. 16, 87
de Jong, P. 73, 93, 132
de Shazer, S. 14, 21, 43, 72
Denborough, D. 40, 50
denial of problem 78–9
Derrida, J. 13
divorce, conflict after 80–4
Dolan, Y. 70
Durrant, M. 20, 91

Edwards, S. 18, 19, 25, 34, 36, 41, 44,
    57, 62, 69, 79, 86, 94, 98, 103
emotions 16–7
ending the session
  feedback 130–6
  homework tasks 124–30
Epston, D. 37
Essex, S. 37, 39, 79
'ever appreciating circles' activity 95
exceptions
  finding 43–9, 62
  not obviously relevant to problem 54–6
  relevant to the problem 52–4
  when there are none 57
externalising conversations 49–52

feedback notes 47, 130–6
finding exceptions 43–9, 62
flexibility 40
Freeman, J. 37

gender 19
goal-setting
    conflicting goals 80–4
    constructive safety goals 65–8
    defining goals 63–5
    denial of problem 78–9
    group miracle questions 76
    in groupwork 148–53
    involving everyone 63–4, 67–8, 73
    learning difficulties and 84
    miracle question 72–8
    preferred futures 70–2
    questions to elicit goals 69–75
    in safe-care plan 120
    shortened circular miracle question 77–8
    'unrealistic' goals 74
Gondolf, E.W. 18
group miracle questions 76
group strengths 94–5
groupwork
    advantages of 144–5
    'Anger Management and Handling
        Conflict' Group 152–3
    difficult group members 153–5
    flexible approach to 155–6
    goal-setting 148–53
    physical environment 146–7
    practice principles 149–53
    rules of the group 147–9
    setting up a group 145–7
    and solution focused approach 144
Gumbleton, J. 37

Hackett, P. 95
Hampton, B. 32
Hanson, B. 157
happiness scale 104–5
Hawkes, D. 74, 155
helplessness 141–2
homework tasks 124–30
hopelessness 141–2
humour 37

inputs/outputs vs. outcomes 64
interests, asking about person's 31–2

Jenkins, A. 29, 34, 36
Jessop, D. 11, 20, 103, 145

Kubicki, A.D. 18

labelling the person 12–3, 14, 33
Lamarre, J. 141
language use 14
learning difficulties 84
leaving violent partner 115–7
Lee, M.Y. 19, 33, 76, 144,
    146, 147, 148, 151
Levy-Peck, J.Y. 144
Lewis, D. 156
likelihood of change, assessing 110–2
Lipchik, E. 16, 18
listening 32–4
Lobovits, D. 37
location of work 40
Luger, C. 37
Luthar, S.S. 25

Madden, B. 16, 87
Maroney, T. 157
Marsh, T.I. 74
metaphors, for violence 29–30
Miller, G. 16
Miller, S. 21
Miller, W.R. 20
Milner, J. 10, 11, 13, 14, 15, 18,
    19, 20, 28, 37, 40, 47, 50, 51,
    52, 54, 55, 66, 70, 72, 73, 84,
    86, 87, 92, 99, 103, 110, 112,
    123, 143, 145, 146, 147, 152
Milwaukee Centre for Brief Therapy 14
miracle question 72–8
motivation 110–2
Murray Parkes, C. 37
Myers, S. 10, 13, 15, 22, 44,
    75, 87, 91, 103

naming the problem 49–52
negativity, effect of 17, 85–8
'not knowing' stance 15
'noticing' (instead of praising) 46
number of sessions 130–1, 137

O'Byrne, P. 15, 18, 47, 50, 70, 143
O'Connell, B. 13, 146
O'Hanlon, B. 16
older people 157

organisational strengths 94–5
outcomes vs. inputs/outputs 64

palliative care 157
partnership, cooperative 34–5
Pichot, T. 150
playfulness 37
post-divorce conflict 80–4
'Power and Control Wheel' 19
praise 45–6, 137, 155
pre-session change question 21
predicting violence 18–9, 21
preferred futures 70–2
pretend tasks 127–8
problem
  denial of 78–9
  'disposing' of 50–1
  instability of 14–5
  'problem saturated descriptions' 86
  separate from the person
      16, 21–2, 49–52
problem-free talk 31–2
progress
  assessment of 112–20
  no change 113–4
punctuality 39

questions
  assessing likelihood of change 110–2
  constructive 34–6
  pre-session change question 21
  scaling questions 102–23

record-keeping
  feedback notes 47, 130–6
  safety assessment process 57–62
Reivich, K. 24
resilience 24–5
Resolutions Approach 37–9
respectfulness 27–30, 39–40, 80
Reuss, N.H. 47, 126
role swapping 36–7
Rollnick, S. 20
Royal College of Psychiatrists 18

safe-care plan 118–20
safety assessment process 57–62
safety pack 114
Saleebey, D. 15, 25
scaling questions 102–23

schools, collaborating with 91–2
Sebold, J. 19
Selekman, M. 24, 137, 146
self-care 105
setting goals see goal-setting
Severin, B. 155
Sharry, J. 16, 76, 87, 98, 145,
      149, 150, 151, 152
Shatte, A. 24
Shennan, G. 144, 150
Shin, S.-K. 144
shortened circular miracle question 77–8
Signs of Safety approach 25–6
'similar but different' stories 37–9
Singleton, T. 11
social constructionism 15
socially isolated people 96–8
Solution Focused Brief
      Therapy (SFBT) 14
solutions focused approaches
  accountability in 19–20
  assumptions of 21–4
  emotions in 16–7
  'not knowing' stance of 15
  overview of 13–21
  resilience and 24–5
sparkling moments activity 96–8
subsequent sessions
  things are better 137–9
  things are the same 139–41
  things are worse 141–3
survival questions 92–4

talking
  about the behaviour 28–9
  people who can't/won't talk 35–7
Teft, P. 20
tenderness, identifying 31–2
terminology, effect of 14
theory, avoid use of 42
therapeutic tyranny 29, 39–40
Truebridge, S. 24
trust 27
Turnell, A. 16, 18, 19, 25, 34,
      36, 37, 39, 41, 44, 57, 62,
      69, 79, 86, 94, 98, 103
'types' of violent people 12–3
tyranny, therapeutic 29, 39–40

Uken, A. 19

violence
   complex nature of 9–13
   predicting 18–9, 21
   solutions focused approaches 13–24
   theories of 11–2
   'types' of violent people 12–3

Watling, T. 82
Wheeler, J. 87

White, M. 49, 86
White, R.J. 18
Wilgosh, R. 74
Wittgenstein, L. 13
Wright, J. 157

Young, S. 94, 144